THE FORGOTTEN SKILLS

THE FORGOTTEN SKILLS

NORMAN MURSELL

illustrated by Rodger McPhail

London
GEORGE ALLEN & UNWIN
Boston   Sydney

**George Allen & Unwin (Publishers) Ltd,
40 Museum Street, London WC1A 1LU, UK**

George Allen & Unwin (Publishers) Ltd,
Park Lane, Hemel Hempstead, Herts HP2 4TE, UK

Allen & Unwin Inc.,
Fifty Cross Street, Winchester, Mass 01890, USA

George Allen & Unwin Australia Pty Ltd,
8 Napier Street, North Sydney, NSW 2060, Australia

First published in 1985

ISBN 0 04 79028 7

Set in 12 on 13 point Garamond by Nene Phototypesetters Ltd, Northampton
and printed in Great Britain
by Butler & Tanner Ltd, Frome and London

Contents

Foreword

Having leafed through the pages of this book the feeling is one of almost unfolding a rural history of great significance, with every story there appears to be another hidden behind it; perhaps a message from bygone days.

Rural life has always had its characters, they have been part of its heritage and it creates these people, usually through the solitary nature of their work, whether hedge-cutter, keeper or blacksmith, to name but a few, and this is a record of some of those people who made this life so rich.

I have no hesitation in commending this book to you.

THE DUKE OF WESTMINSTER

Dedication

Having lived for over fifty years in rural Cheshire, this book is dedicated to the many friends I have made, over the years, who have provided me with so many rich memories. The countryside is a happy place in which to work for people dedicated to their calling, and all my friends have certainly been that! This book is for all of them.

NORMAN MURSELL
1985

1 A view of the farm

With the passing of time many of the rural crafts have disappeared, and with them the people who plied them, the rural characters. It is inevitable that modern methods have displaced much of the work on the land that had probably for centuries been done by hand, and of course in this situation many if not most of the old tools have disappeared too. This is a shame in a lot of ways, for a tractor hasn't the character of a horse, and the men of the farms and country workers in general haven't the same closeness to nature as in the past.

Let's start with the make-up of the present day countryside. Many of the small farms have been absorbed into larger units, apart from the marginal land, where it is impractical to farm with large scale modern machinery. With this increase in the acreage of the average farm has come the increased use of large, modern and expensive machinery: tractors, combine harvesters and other machines which do practically all the sowing, planting, reaping, mowing, draining and hedgecutting required.

1

Even the purely dairy farmer has all the equipment necessary to run the farm with the minimum of labour: there's no spreading of manure by hand, no milking by hand, and no draining or hedging either. All these things mean that farm workers, who perhaps don't like being called farm workers even, rather stockmen and tractor drivers, have much less actual contact with mother nature, they are mostly riding over the land instead of tramping it with their own two feet!

The large estates too have changed so much that there are few employees compared to the old days, and once again there is so much machinery of one sort and another that real contact with the countryside is much less than it used to be.

You will say all this is well known. So it is, but the men who used the tools and practised the old crafts are mostly forgotten. Characters they were, almost without exception, not only the farm workers but the farmers too.

On a large estate with many farms worked by tenants, it was inevitable that some of these men stood out above the rest, but they all had to practise good husbandry or fall by the way. Sometimes there was a certain amount of luck involved as was the case with a farmer shortly after the outbreak of the First World War. Food was starting to be rationed, even basic needs were not completely met, so any luxuries or semi-luxuries were at a premium. This particular man had a small acreage of arable land, growing mainly oats, turnips and mangolds for his stock, but like many yeomen he had an uncanny instinct when it came to making a quid or two. This particular year he had the idea of sowing an acre of onions, a thing unheard of in those days when even the market gardeners shied away from this crop.

Tom Powell, the farmer in question, no doubt knew he was taking a risk, but a calculated one. The normal supply from abroad, from either Spain or France, had ceased. No longer were the 'onion men' seen travelling the towns and villages with strings of onions hanging on their cycles, and of course a large number of able-bodied men were serving their country in the forces. Many of the gardens were being cultivated by women folk who took a year or two to adapt to the routine of cottage gardening, and so, taken all round, onions looked like being at a premium

Today the vast majority of onions are grown from 'sets', a fairly recent innovation, but at the time of the First World War all onions were grown from seed. Growing the sets is practically fool-proof, but onion plants grown from seed are prone to various pests, such as the onion fly which will soon make a mess of a crop when the fly's grubs attack the plant. The plants can also get a fungus disease which can dramatically reduce the yield. By and large Tom Powell had to keep his fingers crossed and hope for a good crop. As it turned out, the weather was kind, there was an absence of pests and the onions grew well and produced a bumper crop. Tom was naturally delighted with the returns from that one acre, for onions were in short supply, and much in demand, and his must have produced a hefty profit.

When asked why he decided to grow onions he always replied 'I thought I would risk it'. Even today some of the old hands in my part of Cheshire, when taking a bit of a chance with something or other say 'Aye, I'll Tom Powell it'. Strange how some things linger on. Of course Tom is no longer around, and apparently that was the one and only time he grew onions!

Perhaps starting a chapter with an 'onion tale' may make you want to cry, but there are no apologies for this, since it is a true story and largely typical of the many chances and risks taken by farmers in the days before subsidies and grants. It was essential that they should be prepared to 'Tom Powell' it.

Cheshire, this being about Cheshire folk, was much more an area of grassland farming than of arable farming. Today of course this has changed. Land that had never been ploughed in living memory is now producing crops of cereal, and even oil-seed rape. The old timers would cast a jaundiced eye over some of the modern practices, for by and large the farming fraternity are conservative folk.

Old Harry Fearnall would have wrung his hands in despair to see some of his treasured pasture land under the plough, even having to turn over a small amount to grow corn during the last war was something he hated having to do. There would have been much discussion in the Scratching Shed, as the farmers called their snug in the local hostelry. Some time after the war Old Harry said it would be ten years before a good grass root had been achieved on this war-time ploughed land. He was proved to be quite accurate, in fact the old lad died before some of the fields on his farm had recovered and achieved their full potential as grazing for cows. Harry maintained that it was no use sowing these new fangled modern grass seeds, aye, they would produce long grass but 'nowt in the bottom'. Two or three years and it wouldn't be worth putting the machine in for hay, according to Harry, who maintained that until the original natural grasses took over again a farm couldn't carry the same number of cows let alone produce that mouthwatering cheese that Cheshire farmers had so long been famous for.

Yes, Harry was a character, but a craftsman when it came to good husbandry; a good employer, a mainstay of the village community and at times a generous man.

He was one of the instigators of the local ex-serviceman's association formed after the nineteen four-teen – nineteen eighteen war, when with other farmers in the area he gave the returning servicemen a slap-up dinner. This dinner is still held annually and one of the men who attended the first dinner still comes to it. Harry of course has long since died, but at least a few know of his good works.

Many farmers years ago seldom changed out of their working clothes, except maybe to go to church on the odd occasion, or perhaps to have a day out at the market and of course to meet their friends in the local taverns, usually after a day at the aforesaid market! Harry, of course, was no exception, and usually wore a 'slop' (brown warehouse coat) tied at the waist with a piece of string, an old battered cap, greasy from hand-milking the cows, leather leggings plastered with mud and cow muck and sturdy boots to keep the water out – no rubber boots in those days. He had a habit of chewing wheat and always had a handful in his pocket. Wheat if chewed and chewed leaves a jelly-like substance akin to chewing gum, and Harry would have a mouthful of this, adding the odd grain or two of wheat occasionally to keep the lump of jelly the required size.

Since Harry was a tenant farmer on Eaton Estate, once or twice during the winter months the second Duke of Westminster would be going round the pits or ponds on his farm in search of snipe. On one such trip the shooting party came across Harry inspecting some field drains, and naturally the Duke stopped to have a word with his tenant. With his fairly ample girth and general appearance and his broad Cheshire dialect, he must have impressed the Duke, for not long after, Harry received a message from the Duke's secretary that his presence was required at the Hall. The instructions were, 'as you are, cow muck and all'. Many times after that Harry had to put in an appearance at Eaton Hall in his working clothes, so the Duke must have got some satisfaction from talking to him, and no doubt quite a few laughs!

A description of Harry Fearnall cannot be complete without the coronation story. He was as has been said, at times a generous man, but naturally, did not like being outdone. At the time of Queen Elizabeth's coronation many plans were being made for the celebrations, and an adjoining farm tenant offered an ox for roasting in the village. When this was brought to Harry's notice, someone asked what he was giving. 'Nowt' was the reply, but there was a twinkle in his eye as he said it. A day or two later he called on the secretary of the Celebrations Fund and told him he wanted to buy everyone in the village a pint of beer on the great day. The secretary was to organise this, giving a ticket to each person over eighteen which could be redeemed for a pint at the local pub, the 'Grosvenor Arms'. When it was pointed out to Harry that not many of the women would drink beer even if it was free, Harry said 'No shorts. If they canny sup a pint they can have half a shandy or a lemonade. I anny selling a bullock to pay for it!' Even so it cost Harry a pretty sum to keep up with his neighbour, or was it the other way round, as Harry had let slip to his neighbour what he intended to do. A canny man was Harry, and one of Cheshire's rural characters.

Another farmer well known for miles around was

Horace Lewis, a rotund man of ruddy complexion, with the gait of one who had spent his life working the land. He was the local 'news-man', gathering and distributing information and gossip, and was highly delighted when he had some tit-bit of information to pass on to anyone he should meet. Of course some of his stories would get distorted, and were often told out of context, the further afield they spread. He was a popular and respected man, a great supporter of all the village events that took place in those days. When hay-making time came around there was always a willing band of workers to help Horace get the harvest in. His was not a large farm, only employing one man, so he was glad to get all the help he could. There was of course the usual supper on those occasions, and his wife would have a laden table for all the helpers to tuck in to. There would be plenty of cheese, and often home-cured ham with onions pickled on the farm, and fresh farm butter and bread. All this was in contrast to some farms where the supper provided would be either bread and cheese or bread and butter, but not bread, butter and cheese, so no doubt Horace's spread partly accounted for his popularity at harvest time. He was a generous yet thrifty farmer making full use of the potential of his farm but at the same time not doing anything that appeared to him to be the least bit extravagant.

When fertilizers started to become available and many farms were using quite large amounts, Horace held back, doubting if the expense involved made them a viable proposition. Eventually he was persuaded by his fellow farmers that their application was well worth while. Thereupon he purchased a few bags to try the job out. Now some of his fields ran along a main road, and others came to a well-used by-road. When the time came to spread the fertilizer, Horace took the bags to a field on a lorry and then gave his man orders to spread the 'chemical', as he called it, for a distance of fifty yards from the highway. To do the job a bucket and saucer were used, and with each step a saucerful of the fertilizer would be spread in an arc over seven or eight yards!

The object of only dressing fifty yards from the highway was to give the impression to passing traffic, and in

6

particular to any farmers, that he was keeping up with the times. In fact Horace kept his land in such good heart that although it was possible to see where the fertilizer had been spread by the darker green of the herbage, apart from the colour there was little if any improvement in the crop.

Being a tenant farmer on an estate Horace would receive a customary brace of pheasant during the shooting season from the landowner. One year the first shoot had been rather early in the season, in fact too early, for although the pheasants were fully feathered, and to all appearances fully grown, they were not really mature, and had not put on the weight of birds shot at the normal time. A brace of these rather immature birds was delivered to Horace, as to all the other tenant farmers on the estate, and by and large they were received gratefully. However, the brace given to Horace seemed to be a bit less in weight than some, and Horace thought he hadn't had quite what he should have.

He talked about the poor quality of the pheasants that year in the pub he visited and complained that 'The brace of them wouldn't make a tidy feed'. This tale, as tales are wont to do, eventually reached the ears of the gamekeeper involved. When the next shooting season came round there was another brace of pheasants for Horace, and of

course, the keeper remembered the previous year's incident and resolved that there would not be a repetition of it. He hunted through all the pheasants in the game larder and picked out the two biggest and heaviest he could find, and after weighing them and putting the weight on a label, duly delivered them. Although Horace had not said anything to the keeper about the smallness of the previous brace of birds, he remarked that it was a good heavy brace when the keeper handed them over. For once the tables had been turned, and nothing further was heard about pheasants for it is very likely that those heavy pheasants were old birds, and not quite as palatable as the younger, though smaller brace of the year before!

Horace was a great man for his food and liked plenty and the best, which was no doubt one reason for his well-filled frame. A friend once gave him a wild duck (mallard) saying, 'That a make a nice feed for you and the missus', and the reply he got was 'Aye, there only wants to be two at the table when there's a duck for dinner.' Whereupon his friend replied, 'Well there is only two of you,' and Horace answered, 'Yes, I know but what I mean is, me and the duck!'

There must be a reason why people with the surname Clark or Clarke are called either 'Nobby' or 'Pop', anyway, a certain farmer of that name had a son who of course was known as 'Young Pop'.

Now this particular Pop was different from most farmers in south-west Cheshire. Practically all the farmers in this area concentrated on milk production and cheese making, but Pop had several side-lines other than making cheese. The cheese-makers all kept pigs to use up the side products of the process, the whey being fed with the meal, but Pop kept pigs to slaughter and sell as meat, this being in the days before slaughter houses had to be licenced. Every week during the winter months a pig would be killed to supply the stall he had every Saturday in Birkenhead market. Pork, before the days of deep freezers was rarely eaten if there wasn't an 'R' in the month, but of course freezers have changed that. Having a stall at the market Pop naturally needed more than just plain pork to make it profitable, so sausages and black puddings were made on the farm, with brawn, the like of which is unobtainable today. The recipe for the puddings and brawn was a family secret, but what a delicious meal they made.

Pop also used to grow an acre or two of potatoes, and quite a 'flat' of turnips or rather swedes, some of these for the market stall. With the eggs from his truly free range hens he usually had a good display of fresh farm produce on his stall for the working people of Birkenhead.

About half the potato crop would be 'earlies' and he would always be amongst the first to start digging them, then as soon as a few drills of potatoes had been cleared, he would start sowing the swedes, and among them he often included a few carrot seeds. Thus Pop had a continuous supply of produce to take to market.

He also grew several acres of corn, nearly always oats in those days, mainly to ensure a rotation of the 'green' crop, but of course providing feed for his stock too. When the time came to cut the corn there would be many rabbits in the crop, and these as well as providing some sport for Pop and his friends who shot them, would often find their way to the market stall. During the winter months one or two ferreting days would be held, and there would be more rabbits for sale, and other farmers would bring him their own rabbits after a ferreting day too. Thus there were conies on the stall most weeks during the winter.

All these activities were so well organised that there never seemed any haste, except perhaps during the hay or corn harvest, when the weather was a much greater factor than it is today.

Pop was always ready for a chat when he met someone he knew, but he had the strange habit of walking off suddenly half way through a sentence, and for no apparent reason. Then, maybe a week or even longer after, if he met that same person again he would without hesitation pick up the conversation where he had left off! Talking to me on one occasion about what he had seen down by a wood that morning, Pop said, 'Rabbits were coming out of that burrow one after the other, none of 'em squealed but just now I saw . . .' and at that point he turned round and walked away. Three or four days later on meeting the

9

author again Pop said without even a good-morning, 'It was a stoat, and not a very big 'un either, looked like a bitch to me.' Of course from the previous conversation I had already guessed the cause of the rabbits' bolting. This was feasible maybe with one person, but no doubt he would talk to quite a number in the course of a week, so goodness knows how he remembered all the conversations he had had, and what about his customers at his market stall!

Fifty years and more ago a lot of casual labour was employed during the busy summer season, but despite the fact that he farmed only eighty or ninety acres, Pop preferred to have his own permanent staff, and employed two full-time men, and also later his son when he left school. Most of this summer labour came over from Ireland, and returned, no doubt with a pocket full of money once the last harvest was gathered, usually the potato crop. Just the odd labourer would over-winter in the area, eking out a living as best he could and spending the nights in hay lofts or in the shippens (cowhouses) where it was warm. Most farmers did not want casual labourers around the buildings once their services were dispensed with, but Pop had a solid sandstone building half a mile from the farm and for many winters one of them made this his night quarters. Pop of course knew about this but would never think of moving him on, 'being a big man in the Church' as he once said. Pop was a sidesman in the Church and attended at least once each Sunday.

Many farms both owner-occupied and tenanted were, and still are in many cases, carried on from generation to generation, and no doubt this must have led to good husbandry. One farm in this category that comes to mind was run by two brothers. Their father had died, and their mother, now aged, looked after the farmhouse with the help of a maid, whilst the brothers did the actual farming, employing a couple of men. Frank and Arthur Denson were not only good farmers but of the breed that was fond of all country sports as well. They were both involved in the shooting on the estate, having been loaders for many years. Perhaps the word 'loaders' in this context needs to be explained. In prewar days when many estates reared large numbers of pheasants it was the custom on a

10

shooting day for the guests to use two guns, and it was the loader's duty to carry the guns for the guest. Whilst the actual shooting was taking place the loader had to load the guns, and ensure that at no time whilst pheasants were coming over did the 'gun' (guest) have an empty weapon in his hands. Sometimes on big days three guns would be used, and then of course two loaders were needed. In either case there was always a lad to carry the cartridges.

The art of loading was a skilled one usually carried out by the farmers from the estate, who naturally were used to handling shot-guns. Most of these farmer-loaders had started as cartridge boys, and were thus familiar with the drill. When a loader retired it was usually one of these lads, the farmers' sons, who replaced him.

Frank 'Farmer' and Arthur 'Tut' after carrying cartridges for a number of years, eventually became loaders, and good at it they were too; all the loaders had to be, when two thousand pheasants were killed in one day.

Many country sports attracted the attention of Farmer and Tut over the years and one which held their interest for more than a decade was coursing. It was rare that a meeting within reasonable travelling distance was without the attendance of the two brothers. Eventually they owned a greyhound or two winning quite a lot of prizes at the smaller meetings and they even had a dog which got through a number of heats in the blue riband of coursing, The Waterloo Cup, before being eliminated.

In the early 1930s they were amongst the first to have a motor car, and were always delighted to help the gamekeeper on the estate where a vehicle would be useful. In the spring when the gamekeepers had to gather broody hens to hatch the pheasant eggs, their offer of help was gladly accepted, since the keepers could go much further afield than usual and this made the task of getting the required number of broodies much easier.

On one such expedition Tut went to the door of a very large well-kept farm and on the appearance of the lady of the house, a well-dressed well-built woman in country tweeds he was heard to say, 'Good evening madam, we are from Eaton Estate, and in search of broody hens to hatch pheasant eggs.' The lady's reply could not be heard, but it

11

was obvious that none were available for Tut turned round and shouted, 'Hey, Farmer, they anny git any' in broad Cheshire dialect!

Whilst on another expedition after broodies, Farmer had arranged to meet a cousin (also a farmer) and one or two friends at a country pub known far and wide as the 'Wet Lanes' since a stream had to be forded to reach it. The crowd duly gathered, one or two keepers and a number of farmers, all enjoying a glass of ale. This ale was brought up from the cellar in a large jug, as was the custom in many rural hostelries in those days, but as it came near to closing time Farmer called for a whiskey all round. The atmosphere was getting a little lively when Tut called for another whiskey apiece, but as Sam Hopley, the landlord went for the bottle, he shouted, 'Hey Sam, bring a jugful', and Sam did! There must have been at least a couple of bottles of mountain dew in that jug. It was in the end emptied, but a number of locals in the party had to help out!

This incident was, of course, before the days of regulations against drinking and driving and before our roads became so congested, and it would be doubtful if another car would be seen on the way home that night. However many of the ditches were deeper than they are now!

Another thing Farmer and Tut loved to do was to help the keepers net rabbits at night and also be with them whilst night-watching for poachers. It was of course to the farming brothers' advantage to help catch the rabbits, as the countryside teemed with them. They were one of the worst farming pests of those days.

Netting rabbits at night can be a lot of fun, but can be and often is hard work as well, so the gamekeepers were glad when the two farmers turned out to help. Today there are few places where the conies are plentiful enough to make taking a net out at night worthwhile. In those far off days it was quite possible to get anything between a hundred and two hundred on a good night.

When working in the area of the Denson farm it was usual for the netting party to go back to the farmhouse when the night's work was done, for a few refreshments, this being usually between two and three in the morning.

The food had usually been prepared by the maid before she retired for the night, and Cheshire cheese sandwiches and a mug of hot tea were most acceptable after the night's work.

On one such nocturnal visit it was found that the maid had not done her duty, probably it was her night off, but of course that did not deter either Farmer or Tut. Farmer was cutting the bread and spreading it with real farmhouse butter, the like of which is unobtainable today, when Tut appeared with a tin of sardines saying, 'We'll have a change from cheese tonight.' Farmer looked up from his task and said, 'I dunna like sardines, fetch that tin of tongue.' Chunnering under his breath, Tut went to change the tins and when he came back with a very large tin of tongue he said, 'You know this is for the party at the week-end Farmer.' At which Farmer replied, 'Aint we having a party now then?'

Great men these two farmers, always moaning about the hard times, but always enjoying country life to the full.

Writing about rabbits brings to mind one particular small farmer who had neither the time, being a one man outfit, nor for that matter, the inclination to deal with the large number of furry animals that were busy day after day and night after night, eating away the corn and grass. He dealt with this problem by employing a local chap for a few weeks to ferret and trap the offending beasties. This fellow was a good trapper and conscientious in his work. He would soon reduce the number of rabbits on the holding, but, as was often the case, the rabbits from the surrounding area would be quick to occupy the more or less empty burrows.

One spring evening the rabbit catcher went to the farm to collect the money due to him, which had been outstanding for some time. The farmer had probably not paid up earlier, knowing full well that more rabbits would be back on his land, and he would then be able to complain that the job hadn't been well done. The pair of them had to take a walk 'To see how many you left', in the words of the farmer. Passing alongside a wood the farmer started to count the number of rabbits to be seen running back into the cover. On reaching the end he turned to the

trapper and said, 'I reckon there's thirty or forty rabbits gone in that wood.' Now there weren't anywhere near that number, but the trapper, not to be outdone replied, 'I'll tell you what Mester, You keep them there "magnifiers" on when we get back to the house and ye count my money out.' So on arriving back at the farm, the bespectacled farmer had little option but to pay the trapper the overdue money.

John Rutter was a character known far and wide not only for his appearance. He was a typical John Bull figure, short of stature, with a ruddy complexion from many years in the open air, and carrying a lot more pounds in weight than his frame was made for. His farm produced some of the best cheese in Cheshire, and for that matter his family still does so, on the same land. He was also a great supporter of all village events, not only those of his own village but many of the surrounding ones as well.

At the local hop, John was always Master of Ceremonies, a task which he excelled at. He wasn't happy unless everyone in the room was on the floor and swinging a leg, and he, despite his weight, was in the thick of it. Many a young country girl was taught to dance by John, for, like so many well-built people he was surprisingly light on his feet. The dances, due to finish at one in the morning, were prolonged by John who would go round with the hat collecting as many coppers as he could, saying, 'It's for the band, I'll ask 'em to play another couple of bars', and it was rare for the dancing to finish before two in the morning.

Not many of these farmers of an earlier era have had sons who have been characters in the same way, but John Rutter is an exception. There do not seem to be as many of these village dances as there used to be, but they have been replaced by posher do's, annual dinners and the like. Now John's son Don is in great demand at these functions. He is not so much an after-dinner speaker as a cross between a comedian and an articulate farmer. 'You'm have heard this one now wunny ye', is a favourite way for him to start, and then he proceeds to tell a real funny story that no one present has ever heard.

This chapter has been about some and only some of the farmers known to me. There are many more, each of whom could probably justify a chapter, but there is much more ground to cover, as we move on to the people these farmers employed, of which there were many, each playing his part in the economy of the countryside and contributing to that really rural life that seems to have largely disappeared.

2 *The labourer's lot*

It is only right that this chapter should be about the men employed by the farmers, the farm-workers. There are of course many other people working in the countryside, but alas nowhere near as many as half a century ago. First let's take a look at some of the people who years ago were called 'farm labourers'.

There were many grades of employees on the farms in the old days. There would be the head cowman, the head waggoner and, where sheep were kept, the head shepherd, each of whom would almost certainly have one or two men under him. Also, where there was arable land, there would be an outside foreman. In the farmhouse itself, very likely there would be a housekeeper and a couple of maids, and of course on most farms in Cheshire at any rate, the cheesemaker. Each of these employees had their part to play in the efficient running of the farm as a whole, but were individually responsible for their own department. There was of course a friendly rivalry between each department, but nevertheless they all had to work as a team. It was a matter of all hands to work when

16

the haymaking season arrived, for in prewar days and earlier everything was done by manual labour. There were no balers to tie the crop of hay in neat bundles and no elevators to carry the hay on to carts.

Most farms started cutting the hay in the very early morning, just before dawn. Then it had to be turned after a couple of days or so, according to the weather, and although machines gradually came onto the scene, the early ones were not very efficient. Should the weather be on the damp side, the 'swath turner' would not turn over the 'swaths' cleanly, and so many farmers preferred to do it by hand rather than use 'that new fangled machine'. On one, admittedly large farm I once saw thirty two men at this task, and although it was a large field, a gang that size soon had the job done.

Something that has long disappeared from the country scene is the sound of the waggoners taking their horses to the farm to start the day's work. Many a cottager relied on the clip clop of the horses' feet plodding down the lanes and roads to wake him during the summer months.

One such chap, Ted Walker, could be heard calling his horses (most waggoners looked after two) with a loud, 'Come on me lads, let's be having you'. They would come straight away to the field gate where Ted was waiting, and once their head collars were in place, Ted could be heard saying to his charges in a loud voice, 'Whey, woa, back, come on me lads.' He would repeat the phrase time and again and it could be heard above the rattle of the horses' feet on the country road.

Each waggoner or 'horseman' was responsible for loading his own vehicle, be it cart or lorry, and to do this with loose hay was an art. Before carting the hay commenced, the crop had been turned, rowed in, and then put into 'cocks' ready for loading. Now if these 'cocks' or small piles of hay, hadn't been built correctly, the task of loading was much more difficult, for when an attempt was made to pick the pile of hay up with a 'pikel' (pitchfork), it just fell apart. A properly made cock could be lifted cleanly at one go, and by remaining intact made it a much easier job to load a cart.

Ted Walker was an expert at most jobs where horses

17

were involved, but the sight of a load of hay going out of the field after Ted had loaded it was worth seeing. The load would be just wide enough to pass through any gates on the route to the farm, and the sides were as straight as a house wall as Ted always said. There would hardly be a wisp of hay shed all the way to the farm, a sure sign of a good loader. With maybe two men pitching the load to him, Ted would work round the vehicle, and on completion of each round, put two or three pikels' full in the middle of the load, these being the 'binders' whose purpose was to keep the load firmly in place. Normally each waggoner unloaded his own load, but anyone who had the task of unloading Ted's had no problem as long as he worked round the load in a clockwise direction.

Many men were as efficient as Ted, but few had his expertise in so many of the tasks involving the motive power of those days: horses. From ploughing, drilling, mowing, to the carrying of the crops, Ted excelled at them all. It was hard work and he often worked long hours, but with the disappearance of characters like him the countryside has lost so much. A noisy stinking tractor is no comparison with a well-trained team of horses, but as horses are no longer a viable proposition, we are stuck with the mechanical ones.

The modern stockman (he doesn't seem to be called a cowman these days) does not seem to be as close to his charges as in days gone by. High yield is all that seems to matter in these modern times, and once a cow fails to come up to the required output, it will be changed for a beast with a higher yield. The financial aspects and the viability of farming methods today are not going to be discussed here, but this approach does seem to have made a lot of difference to the men employed, in this particular context, the cowman.

Many of the old timers would bring the cows in for milking on their way into work, for walking to work was the rule. In some parts of the country, the footpaths made by the farm-workers have now been claimed as public footpaths!

Milking the stock twice a day by hand was a time-consuming business, but in many cases the cowman had to help out with other jobs as well. One such chap, Sam by name, had been helping the other men on the farm to thin mangolds, but left when 'cow-time' arrived. When the cows were tied up in the shippens and all the milking staff were assembled, Sam suddenly realized he had lost his wallet. Now it was somewhat unusual for farm-workers to carry wallets in those days, so Sam got little sympathy when he claimed that he had over fifty pounds in that wallet. 'Bet the missus dinna know', and 'Dassent you leave it at home', were some of the comments Sam received, but nary an offer to help him look for the missing cash holder. Fifty pounds was a small fortune when a week's work only produced under two pounds, so no doubt Sam's work-mates were rather sceptical, at least about the amount Sam claimed to have lost. However, when milking was finished, Sam retraced his steps of the afternoon, and by good fortune found the missing wallet. He took it to work the next morning and went to great lengths to show his workmates that it did really contain the amount claimed, but that was the last time the wallet was seen. Sam must have found a safe hiding place for it, since he evidently did not want to leave it anywhere within reach of his wife and family!

Sam was a prudent man, for it must have taken him many years to have amassed that small fortune. He was probably saving for his old age, for it was a struggle for many old timers when they could no longer work. Many of them were forced to work well into their seventies, not giving up until ill-health forced them to do so, when it often fell to their own grown-up married children to look after them.

The shepherds were men who had been born in 'sheep country', for example the hill country and marginal land of Wales. Not a particularly large number of sheep were kept in this part of Cheshire, but there were however several full-time shepherds. Their job, like others on the land, could not be done properly by watching the clock. They had to be with the flock when a job was to be done no matter what the time of day or night. This of course particularly applied during the lambing season, and at that time some shepherds would almost live in huts amongst their flocks. Their wives would often bring them their meals and even on occasion help with the lambing, for certain farmers would give a small amount to the shepherd for each lamb reared, and every penny counted in those days!

The bleating of the lambs was a sure sign that spring was on the way, and they always were and still are an attraction for children of all ages. Maybe it is their association with religion and Our Lord, who knows. One thing is certain: many shepherds have a fine turn of phrase that sometimes unfortunately verges on the blasphemous.

One shepherd, or rather apprentice shepherd, whose name was George Howard, had only just started work on the home farm of a large estate. He had been told to take a flock of sheep to a fresh field, and to do this he had to travel some distance along one of the drives to the Hall. His boss said to him, 'George, now be careful. If you see a car or a horse coming, get those sheep onto the drive side quickly, for it is sure to be the Duke'. Well George, having only recently started his new job was particularly alert, and sure enough heard the approach of a motor car. A quick order to the dog at his heel and the flock was soon on the wide grass verge. The car came slowly past, and on seeing the driver who was wearing a hard hat, George doffed his cap. 'That's the Duke,' thought George, and was really pleased that he had seen his employer, even though he was only passing in a car. Now cars weren't very plentiful in those days, so George was convinced it could only be the Duke. What he didn't know was that the head gamekeeper was a sick man, and the Duke had supplied a car and driver to take the semi-invalid about.

Of course when George returned to the sheep yard, he was full of the story of how he had met the Duke on the drive and went to great lengths to describe the car and the driver. 'The Duke was in a grey suit and wearing a hard hat, a real smart gentleman he was,' said George. Of course the head shepherd realised that it hadn't been the Duke, for he rarely wore a hard hat, preferring to wear a battered old trilby, and in any case he happened to know that the Duke was in Norway! No doubt the keeper's driver was amused to have a shepherd boy doff his cap to him!

The shepherds had to be, and still are, highly skilled men, although life is much easier on the lowland sheep areas than on the mountainous areas of this country. There has undoubtedly been some progress in the way a flock of sheep is cared for, but by and large they still have to be handled in the traditional way. The sheep have to be sheared and although hand clippers have been replaced by power driven ones, the same old skill is needed in actually taking the fleece of wool from the animal. Foot rot still occurs when the sheep are on heavy land during wet weather, and the dipping in a strong disinfectant is still an essential part of a flock's welfare. No doubt some of the chemicals used for foot rot, dipping, worming and so on, have been improved, but there can be but little change in the way each sheep is handled individually. Tractors are also available to transport feed and other necessities such as fencing, but by and large the same old methods prevail today.

The sheep dogs always play an important part in a shepherd's life. Many old hands were experts at training dogs to a very high standard, particularly those in hilly country, where the dog often had to work at a great distance from his handler. On the lowland sheep farms, where the sheep are fenced in, in comparatively small areas, the shepherd can see their every move, and thus the dog relies more on his master. The sheep dog trials held in many areas annually are always a great attraction to the public and demonstrate so well the skills required. The television programme *One Man and His Dog* shows very clearly one side of a shepherd's life, that of working his dogs, but of course the best dogs in the country are probably competing in a show like that, and not all of them are owned and trained by shepherds. Most working shepherds are content to have a good faithful dog that is capable of doing all that is required of it in its own particular situation, and these dogs are well loved.

Many years ago a shepherd had been taking some sheep off meadow land because there were signs of an imminent flood, the nearby river being bank-full. He was pleased that he had achieved his object before the meadows flooded, for water was already seeping through the high restraining banks, but he now had to return to the farm some distance away. He rode his bike along a drive through the estate that was also liable to flood, and arrived at the lower part of the drive to find that the water was already several inches deep. He pedalled on, with his faithful dog running alongside his cycle, for this was the only way back to the farm without doing a four mile detour. The further Owen went, the deeper the water got, and it was soon pouring over the drive at a rate of knots. Then with about forty yards to go there came a surge of rushing water at least a foot high. The speed and force of this torrent swept Owen's bike from under him, and he had great difficulty regaining his feet. His one concern then was to gain dry land, and for the moment he forgot his faithful dog.

Eventually Owen struggled the forty yards to safety, and only then did he realise that his dog was not with him. He called and called, thinking that the dog would have swum to safety but to no avail. By now more estate workers had come along the drive, only to find their progress barred by the water, and to be confronted by Owen in a bedraggled state, shouting pitifully for his dog.

It was fortunate that these men arrived when they did, for Owen in his shocked state started back into the rushing muddy water in search of his dog. Several men had to follow him in and restrain him or without a doubt there would have been a human tragedy as well as a canine one. The poor dog was carried away by the rushing water, and no doubt was eventually exhausted and drowned. No dog, no matter how strong or faithful could fight such a force, but it was some time before Owen could be persuaded to leave, hoping against hope that his dog would reach safety.

By the very nature of their job many farm-workers had a number of skills which were most essential on the smaller farms where maybe only a couple of men were employed. Most of their tools were, by today's standards, what I suppose can only be called primitive, and each worker often had his own particular choice of tool to do a specific job.

It was a marvellous sight to see, say, half a dozen men in a large field, thinning turnips or maybe mangolds. The field had been ploughed, almost certainly by one man using a single furrow plough, and then ridged up with a 'ridging' plough. In due course the 'green crop' seed would be sown on the top of the ridge, using a seed 'barrow', which required two men, one of whom would be leading the horse. The seed would germinate, usually in about a week to ten days, depending on the weather. In warm, humid or showery weather, the seedlings would soon grow, and that was when all the farm staff were employed in the job of thinning. This served two purposes, the main one being to single out the seedlings, giving them a chance to grow and produce a heavy crop. In fact in some parts of the country the job was called 'singling' not 'thinning'. The other object of this laborious job, was to destroy the weeds, and a day with a good warm sunshine was usually chosen to get amongst the green crop.

The main tool used for thinning was a hoe, a draw hoe not one of the dutch type so popular with gardeners. The name 'draw' gives an indication of the way this tool was used. It was placed behind the row of seedlings and drawn towards the operator, thus uprooting the young plants,

23

exposing the roots to the sun and causing them to wither and die.

A skilled man could go at almost walking pace up a drill thinning the row of seedlings with deft strokes, leaving single plants approximately ten inches or a foot apart. At the same time he would draw the hoe along each side of the drill to destroy any weeds that might be present or ready to germinate. Frequently the farmer would be working with his men, setting the pace, to ensure the job was done as rapidly and efficiently as possible.

One old farm worker, Edwin Jones, a man who had spent his whole working life on the land, would not be paced at this task, or at any other for that matter. When the gang reached the end of the row Edwin always went to sit under the hedge, despite the fact that the farmer and the other men just turned round and started back down another drill. Edwin would get out his baccy tin and proceed to cut up a pipeful of twist tobacco, teasing the twist out and rubbing it in his gnarled hands before filling the bowl of his short-stemmed pipe. Matches were produced and the pipe duly lit. 'Twist' used to be a dark strong tobacco, hardly obtainable today, which often only got going satisfactorily after several attempts and a number of matches. Once he had 'a full head of steam' as he called, it, he would start up the next drill some fifteen or twenty yards behind his employer and workmates, but no matter, it was rare indeed for him to reach the other end of the field behind the others, and he would beat them by a 'short head'.

Such was his skill with the draw hoe, that despite what appeared to be careless swipes with the tool, he soon caught the rest of the gang up, for they were often less experienced. His employer never discouraged Edwin from stopping for a pipe of baccy, knowing full well that he was doing a good job, quickly and probably better than the other men.

Sometimes a farmer would set this task piecework, at so much a drill, especially after a showery warm spell when the weeds had flourished, which of course made the job rather slower. There would be quite a bit of haggling over the price, for the work was usually done in the evening after a normal day's work was finished. The men were naturally glad of the extra money, for large families were the order of the day and even an extra shilling made a difference. Despite the fact that the job was done at so much a drill it was usually done to the same standards as in working hours; it had to be or another time the farmer would reduce the price!

There aren't so many green crops grown today. Despite the fact that some modern machinery is available it is a pretty labour intensive crop, and a change in cattle feeding methods makes it no longer necessary. Ox or cow cabbage used to be at one time a very popular feed for cows, and many acres of it were grown. A lot of labour was required to handle this crop and gradually it dropped out of favour in most areas. The cabbage plants were usually bought in, literally by the thousand, for it took a lot to plant a ten acre field. The bundles of plants were thrown under the hedge and maybe a week later, when all the leaves had turned yellow, the field would be planted up. There was of course an art to this planting. The men worked in pairs, one with a spade and the other carrying a bundle of plants. The spade was thrust into the ground on the ridge of the prepared drill by one man, and the other man pushed a plant into the ensuing cut in the soil. The spade was withdrawn, a heavy foot firmed the plant in the cut, and a measured stride taken, for the next plant to go in. A good pair of men could literally go at walking pace at this task. I wonder if the term 'clodhopper' comes from this seasonal job? A day or two later, if the weather was dry, all that could be seen up the field, was a line of yellowed stalks, but come September it was a different tale, the soil would be invisible, the field just one mass of huge cabbages. Old Edwin always said that if you made members of the cabbage family fight to survive, you always got a better crop. This certainly seemed true of the ox cabbage, but I don't know a gardener who would like to see his cabbages just yellow stalks!

All the green crops were carried off the field by horse and cart in those far off days; the turnips and mangolds pulled and topped and thrown in rows for the waggoners to load. There was a difference in the treatment of these

two. Both the tops and the roots of turnips were trimmed off using a special tool with a knife edge and a hook at the end. The hook was used to pull the turnip out of the ground before trimming. When pulling mangolds a similar tool was used without the hook, for mangolds must not have their surface broken or rot sets in. Thus turnips when pulled would be loaded onto the cart using an often three pronged pikel (pitchfork) but the mangolds had to be thrown onto the cart by hand, a back-breaking business, particularly on a cold wet day. When the men hauled these crops to the farm, at least in the case of turnips and cabbages, it was the custom to throw a cabbage or a turnip or two into each cottage garden as they passed and Ted Walker, the waggoner mentioned earlier, would frequently make a detour to ensure no one was missed out.

There were often very heavy crops in those days, despite the fact that no fertilizers were used, apart from what is really a mineral, lime, a load or two being used on the farms at infrequent intervals. In good seasons the crops would be terrific, with cabbages eighteen inches across (ox cabbages are a flat topped variety) and mangolds that would literally sit on a bucket.

In one such bumper year the farm-hands were discussing these topics in the local hostelry one evening when a hand from a distant farm came in. He was asked if they had been carrying mangolds. 'Aye', said Ellis. 'What sort of a crop?' he was asked. 'Pretty fair,' said Ellis. 'Oh good,' said his interrogator, pulling Ellis's leg of course, 'We've got a crop that a' take some beating, it takes two of us to throw a mangold on the cart.' 'That's nowt,' was Ellis's reply, 'Boss had to get the cross cut [saw] out, 'for us could make a start!' Some crop – some men!

During the winter months there were many tasks for the farm-workers that could not have been done earlier, even had there been time, for the hedges were in full leaf, and it was rare to cut a hedge when still in its summer clothing, in those days. The attention to drainage had to wait until there was water in the ditches, for a good man needed nothing but his eyes, trusty tools and maybe an instinct born of long practice, to drain a field, which he probably did better than anyone today using modern methods.

Before the days of combine harvesters, a corn crop was harvested with a 'binder'. Now a binder saved a lot of work for as the corn stalks were cut they passed over a canvas and wood framework, and were then tied in bundles (sheaves). An earlier machine, the reaper, only cut the standing corn, leaving it in orderly rows across the field. This of course had to be tied in bundles and 'set up'. It was some task tying eight or ten acres of corn by hand, into sheaves, but most farm labourers on arable farms were adept at this.

With a few quick twists of a handful of straight straw and a doubling over of the heads of grain, a band was made. This would be done by the farm-worker as he shuffled along the rows of cut corn. Almost invariably by the time the band was made, there was enough of the crop at his feet for him to slip the band under it, and with another quick twist tie it into a bundle (sheaf).

There were nearly always four, five or six men working together in a field, and as they tied the bundles, they stood them on end, with the grain to the sky forming a 'stook'. Usually eight sheaves formed a 'stook' and these stooks were so well built, albeit swiftly, that it took very heavy or prolonged rain to wet more than the outside.

These cutting and 'stooking' operations took place before the corn was really ripe (hard) so it was quite a while before it was fit to be carried to the stackyard. At least fourteen days were needed to harden the grain, as the old farmers used to say, 'The church bells must ring over it thrice'. These predictions were not always accurate of course, as sometimes there were two church services on a Sunday!

No farmer liked to have his crop of corn still fast at one end, when it was almost ripe, for the cutting operation would shed a lot of the grain, and the resultant yield be reduced. Naturally quite a lot of grain fell from the ear when the carrying of the crop began, but most of this would happen when the sheaves were thrown on to the carts and lorries. As they were stacked heads to the sky, when they were lifted with a pikel and thrown onto the vehicle they landed on the heads of grain, and some was knocked out. This dislodged grain was not wasted, for it

27

was swept off the cart when the load was stacked, and mostly used to feed the poultry that roamed the farmyard.

There was a skill in 'pitching' a load. Some men, Ellis Jones is one who comes to mind, could handle the sheaves so skilfully that no one was needed on the cart to put them in place. With a man like Ellis each side of the cart, and a lad leading the horse, it was amazing how soon a cart was loaded, and for that matter, how soon a field was cleared!

Many of these corn crops were stored in 'stacks', (even a haystack is now practically a thing of the past), and it could be many months before the mobile threshing box came to thresh the grain. This being so, it was essential that these stacks were made waterproof by thatching. This thatching was of course very different from the thatching of a building, one reason for this being that it was of a temporary nature. Wheat straw was usually the material used, and many farm hands could make an excellent job of it, ensuring that none of the winter rains could penetrate and rot the hard-won crop. Few tools were used for this task: a pikel to pitch the selected straw to the top of the stack, a billhook to sharpen the pegs to hold the straw in place which were usually made of hazel, and often a pair of hand sheep-shearers to trim off the loose ends. It was a grand sight to see a number of these stacks in a farmyard, often round in shape, and in many cases raised off the ground on 'mushrooms'. The mushrooms were devices to keep the rats and mice from devouring the grain, and ruining the straw, being designed so that even if the rodents climbed the stalk of the mushroom, they could not climb any further. In many ways it is a pity that these things are not seen today, unless as ornaments in a cottage garden or in some old painting or photograph of a rural scene.

A lot of skill was needed to build these stacks or ricks as they were called in some parts of the country. A square or rectangular one was difficult enough, but the round ones on mushrooms needed that extra bit of know-how. To start with, the mushroom tops were criss-crossed with timber, often wind-blown branches then smaller brushwood was placed on top. This was the base that was built on, but the most difficult part was making the stacks circular, which they really were. The stacker would start round the outside, and keep going round and round, with the odd inner circle to act as a binder. Eventually he would arrive at the required height and then reduce the size of the circle, finishing off with a pointed roof. Very often a well-made stack was almost impervious to rain, but the prudent farmer had it thatched nevertheless, for a severe storm could easily dislodge the sheaves and let the elements in.

Many people will have seen pictures of farm labourers' wives in the corn-fields after the crop has been cleared. These women, often accompanied by their children, were carrying out the time-honoured custom of 'gleaning'. Gleaning was searching the fields for heads of grain that had been cut off during the process of harvesting, and it was considered a perk of the people employed on the farm. No doubt some of the men who operated the horse-drawn reaper made sure some heads were cut off the standing crop, to make it worth while for their wives to go gleaning! But no doubt the work was also watched closely by the farmer.

This gathering of heads of grain was at one time an important part of rural economy. Almost all country dwellers kept a few head of poultry and, no doubt the heads of grain gathered from a field of stubble were a great help in feeding the egg producers on the back yard. The shed grain was not wasted for the farmer often bought in a number of goslings to feed on the stubbles, and these needed very little more feed until just before Christmas, and contributed profitably to the farm economy. A lad usually had the task of taking out the geese in the morning and bringing them back in the evening, for reynard loves nothing better than a plump goose!

The stacks or ricks had of course eventually to be threshed, and in far off days, this was done by a travelling threshing machine, although in some parts of the country where there were large arable farms the farmer would own his own equipment.

It was a dusty dirty job working on the threshing 'box' and at times quite dangerous too. Quite a number of men were needed to keep things running smoothly. There would be two men on the stack to throw the sheaves to the man cutting the bands and feeding the box, the sheaves having to be fed in grain-head first. Then there had to be one or sometimes two men to bag and carry away the grain as it came out of the shute, another man to move the straw, and another to remove the chaff, which made six or seven hands at least. It was quite a big operation on a small farm, but one farm always helped out another, and there were usually a couple of men who travelled with the 'box'; the driver of the steam traction engine which supplied the power, and an odd-job man who would turn his hand to anything.

Many areas of the country did not build the stacks on these mushrooms often because there was no suitable stone in the district to make these unusual and attractive blocks. Where mushrooms were not used the practice was to form a base of wind-blown timber directly on the ground and for some reason unknown to me, these stacks were usually rectangular. As the grain was close to the ground it was inevitable that the stacks were frequently infested with rodents, rats and mice, much to the displeasure of the farmer. There were no chemicals to deal with these pests in those days, and as the destructive creatures had a large mass of straw to hide and breed in, they were almost impossible to control.

The disturbance of threshing time made it possible to take a toll of the unwanted guests. As work on the stack progressed the rats and mice became uneasy and in due course started to show themselves on the outside of the stack. It was a universal custom at this point to encircle the stack with small-mesh (usually half inch) wire netting. This checked the rats and mice when they eventually made a bid for freedom, and they could then be dealt with.

A lot of fun was had as the rats and mice appeared. Men and lads would be waiting for them with sticks and any wieldable objects, ready to deal a hefty blow and crush the life out of the pests. One old lad always grabbed a spade and joined in the fray saying, 'I can't dang well miss 'em with this', but everyone else had to keep well clear of him as he wielded his weapon with great gusto. One or two men or lads always remained outside the wire which was about three feet in height, for rats and mice are both pretty

30

active, especially when scared, and could quite easily climb the wire netting.

No doubt many a bruise was caused by the flaying sticks, but in all the excitement no one complained. There were other dangers inherent in the old method of threshing: men have been known to be stuck with a pitch-fork, accidentally of course, and the man feeding the machine often cut his hands on the very sharp knife he had to use. I also know of one case where a man slipped into the drum that threshed the grain, and damaged one leg so badly that it had to be amputated. Charlie Mellor was the man's name, and despite those injuries of many years ago he is still alive. Although sadly handicapped, he carried out his duties, and ran a farm of some size for a long time until his retirement a fair while ago.

A thought has just struck me about rat catching at threshing time: what would the 'antis', those people who clamour against blood sports, have had to say?

There were of course no antis, at least not vociferous ones in those days, for the farmers had to deal with pests as best they could, even if their methods involved some cruelty. Rat poisons and rodent operatives control the pests these days, but who can say that their methods are any less cruel? It was not at all unusual for several hundred rodents to be killed when one stack was being threshed,

31

so you can see how important it was to do this. A large amount of grain would have already been spoilt, but imagine the damage such a horde would do after breeding for the twelve months leading up to the next harvest!

3 *Inside the farmhouse*

Now we come to the inside staff, those employed within the farmhouse, indispensable assistants to the farmers' wives. For some reason, particularly on large estates, farmhouses were of great dimensions, often having eighteen or twenty rooms and large rooms at that. It is a bit difficult to know why they should be so large. Of course families were bigger in those days and there had to be accommodation for the servants, but so many servants wouldn't have been needed in a smaller house! Was a large well-staffed farmhouse really what people today call a status symbol or was it a necessity? In any case it created work for rural lasses who normally had no difficulty finding a job, and almost always 'lived in', thus taking some pressure off a home struggling to make ends meet.

If a girl went to work in a farmhouse straight from the village school (children left school at fourteen in prewar days) she did all the menial tasks, such as scrubbing the floors, and hard work that was too. She would be down on her hands and knees with plenty of hot soapy water, a hand-held scrubbing brush and a vast area of rough tiles in front of her. For a young girl it must have been a heartbreaking introduction to working life. The farmer's wife was often a hard taskmaster and slipshod work rarely

33

escaped her searching gaze. Despite the fact that all floors were hard-scrubbed regularly, often daily, they had to be done thoroughly.

After a while working in the house, a maid had to learn to milk (where milk was the main produce) and she eventually turned out morning and night for this arduous task, for all milking was done by hand. Six o'clock in the morning was the starting time and the second milking of the day would begin maybe around four in the afternoon, which meant that it would be half past five or six o'clock before the day's labour would be finished. The girls were quite happy with their lot and probably enjoyed the milking sessions, for it was then that they had a chance to talk to the farm-workers' wives. It was the custom for the wives of the men who worked the land to turn out twice a day to milk, and although the money they received was a mere pittance it all helped the household budget. They also probably were glad to get together and to be out of their often isolated cottages.

There would naturally be much talk of the goings-on in the nearest village, about any 'hatching, matching or dispatching' (births, marriages or deaths) that had taken place, for practically all country folk knew at least the apparent business of all the other folk in the area.

Most of the young girls eventually married young chaps who worked on the land and often had large families and continued to milk at the farm where their husbands worked. One such lady already had several children, and another was due. She continued to milk each night and morning until she had to leave the evening milking early one day as the birth was imminent. During that evening the child was born and the next morning the lady was back at the farm at her usual time to milk, leaving her new-born in the care of the eldest daughter. They were tough folks in those days. That particular lady reared eight children and lived to a ripe old age!

Inside the farmhouse there was in most cases an older maid who was in charge of the younger girl or sometimes girls, and who was responsible for the household chores. The scrubbing and cleaning and polishing was all done by the youngest or latest to join the household, while

34

the senior maid did the lighter tasks, looking after the bedrooms and so on. Monday was always a heavy day in the household week as it was washing day. There was neither a modern day washing machine, nor laid-on hot water. Early on a Monday morning the wash boiler would be lit, and with much coaxing and stoking of the fire, the water was brought to the boil. As soon as the water was hot enough, the task would begin. There were no modern washing powders with their so-called bio-chemical properties. Sometimes flaked soap was available to make the suds in the 'dolly tub', if not, a block of soap would be scraped with a knife and the scrapings added to the hot water in the tub. The articles to be washed were placed in the soapy water and then the hard work would begin. The clothing would be pummelled with an implement called a 'dolly' (hence the name dolly tub). This implement was made of wood and pretty heavy, with five pegs on a circular base and a strong wooden handle which had a crosspiece, to enable a twisting action to be used to stir the washing. In due course, the articles were removed from the soapy water and rinsed in another tub or in a sink. Any persistent stains or dirt had to be removed by hand, using more soap and a 'washboard'. This type of washboard was later used by the early skiffle groups!

A further rinse and the clothes were hung out to dry, which was fine on a nice breezy day in the summer, but imagine the problems that arose on a dreary wet, winter's Monday morning! All of this was real hard labour, for a farm is not the cleanest place to work and some of the stains were pretty persistent, needing much pummelling on the washboard!

Then of course the piles of ironing had to be done on the Monday evening if this was possible, and as it was completed it would be put on an airer which hung from the kitchen ceiling. This airer was on pulleys fastened to the ceiling and when full was hoisted up above head height, to catch the hot air rising from the kitchen range! Often on a Monday it was quite late before the work was done, and no doubt it was not a day the farmhouse maids looked forward to.

Linen and clothing of course, needed to be repaired

from time to time, and everything was of such good quality in days gone by that it was repaired again and again. It was not the fashion conscious and throw-away world we live in today. Even the maids' dresses or uniforms would last for a very long while, and any minor tears or worn parts were repaired. It was the custom for a seamstress to travel a given area, staying a few days or maybe a week at each farm. She would go through all the household linen and clothing and do what repairs were needed. Maybe the farmer's wife would have a new dress or two made, or perhaps a new set of curtains.

It would be probably six months before the seamstress made another visit, and of course by that time there would be more work for her nimble fingers. These 'ladies', for they were treated as one of the family, had a pretty busy life, but were probably as well off as any of the working country folk. They had no accommodation to worry about, no food bills to pay, and their transport was laid on in the form of a horse and trap from one farm to another, so the pay they received could practically all be saved. No doubt clothes would be no problem, since cast-off dresses from the various farmers' wives would be adapted, and put to good use. It was a job well suited to middle-aged spinsters, which most of them were.

A lot of diplomacy was no doubt needed, for tittle-tattle from a farm recently visited would not have been well received, if it returned to its source, and the seamstress would probably have been given no work at that holding again.

The maids usually had to do their own needle work, and many of them were very skilled at it, for long winter evenings gave them plenty of time to practise. I know a lady called Alice, for instance, who started her working life as a maid on a farm, graduated to the rank of cheesemaker (of which more anon) and still, although no longer young, makes many exquisite articles, crochet table cloths for instance, which are really works of art. Her early days as a farmhouse maid gave her an opportunity to learn a skill that she has never lost, and with it she has provided heirlooms for her grandchildren and great grandchildren.

One item which was in common use on all farms was

the 'rough apron'. This was an apron made from a closely woven hessian sack, which was used for the dirtier jobs about the house, such as cleaning and blackleading the kitchen range. The aprons were simple in construction but each maid would add her own individual touch, such as a waistband of a brightly coloured material, or an embroidered flower. This of course was done so they could identify their own aprons, for otherwise one piece of hessian looks very much like another!

Hessian sacks had many uses besides containing grain. Some of the thicker bags, 'meal bags', which were made of a much closer weave almost like canvas, came in very useful to protect people from the weather. The meal bags were quite large, almost three feet in length and made to hold a hundredweight. By pushing one of the closed corners into the other, and then placing the cone thus formed over the head, the wearer could protect himself from the rain. The milk maids would don them when crossing from the shippen to the dairy on a wet day, the shippen being the cow house where the milking stock, tied up in stalls, was fed and milked.

Many farms had the dairy attached to the house, and it could be some distance away from where the cows were milked, so it was often the maids' job to carry the full buckets of milk across the farmyard. Large buckets they were too, holding about four gallons, and a couple of them would weigh above eighty pounds, so a 'yoke' was used. The yoke was made from a piece of timber, usually beech, about a foot longer than the width of an average shoulder, from the ends of which were suspended chains with hooks to engage in the bucket handles. The chains were adjustable so that should a short person be using it, the buckets could be held clear of the ground. Making light of heavy work? Hardly, for struggling over an often cobbled yard, with two full buckets of liquid was not to be preferred to sitting under a cow milking, even if the cow did kick on occasions!

Today of course, farms have a milking parlour, where one man can milk a whole stock of cows in a little over an hour, and the milk is piped to the dairy and stored in a stainless steel tank at a thermostatically controlled temperature. There are no hefty dairy maids on the farms these days, but no wonder these girls turned out to be well-developed in 'wind and limb'.

Earlier in this chapter I mentioned cheesemakers. Now in many parts of the country farms would make their own cheese, which was usually sold to 'Cheese Factors' for general distribution. In Cheshire, where my recollections are drawn from, most farms made cheese for it was in the main, a milk producing county. The smaller holdings mostly sold the liquid milk and those a bit larger would only make cheese during the summer, when with plenty of lush grass about, milk production was high.

Quite a few of the farmers' wives made the cheese on the farm, but particularly on the larger places, a full-time cheesemaker was employed, being in most cases, a maid who had progressed through the various ranks of domestic employment and eventually attended an Agricultural College and graduated in the art of making cheese. The position of cheesemaker on a farm was a coveted one, for although it was one of great responsibility, it was also one of privilege. For instance, whereas the maids often had to wear a maid's dress at all times, the cheesemaker would wear normal clothes, except of course when actually making the cheese. The white apron and other clothing would be provided by the cheesemaker herself, and it was her responsibility to look after it and launder it. In many ways she was a person apart, although of necessity she had to have a good relationship with all the other persons in the household.

The position of cheesemaker was distinguished by the fact that at meal times she would eat at the same table as the farmer, his wife and family, but any other servants in the household would be at a separate table at the other end of the kitchen. This table was often a white wood scrubbed affair, bereft of table cloth, whereas the farmer's table would be covered with a white starched linen cloth, leaving no doubt of the relative positions of the household. Now of course all farms weren't run on this basis, but this was the general rule. Often if the farmer or his wife were particularly 'careful' or downright mean, the servants might have for supper for instance, either bread and butter, or bread and cheese, but not bread and butter and cheese! This was a rather stingy attitude when butter as well as cheese was often made on the premises.

As I said, cheesemaking was a highly skilled job and it was important from the farmer's point of view that each day's production should be of the highest quality. So I will endeavour to describe the main stages in the making of cheese. The milk, when brought in from the milking sheds, was put through a strainer to remove any trace of cow-hair, hay-seeds or any other impurity, for these were pretty plentiful in the buildings of prewar days. It was normal to make cheese in the morning, so the previous night's milk had the morning's production added to it before the process could begin.

The milk was put into a double-skinned receptacle which could hold up to two hundred gallons or even more. To begin the process of changing milk into cheese, steam or hot water was let into the space between the two skins of the 'vat' and this heated the milk to a given temperature (approximately 86°F). When the correct temperature was reached a 'starter' was added, and the milk stirred to give an even distribution. This starter was usually made on the farm and the easiest way to describe it

is as sour milk. Of course it is really a bacterial culture which starts an action close to fermentation.

After something like two hours, 'rennet' was added, to the order of about an ounce to forty gallons of milk. This caused the milk to coagulate, and the milk then turn into one mass, not unlike the 'junket' of childhood days, which was milk with rennet added! The time taken to create this curd varied often from day to day. There were many factors that affect it such as the weather and even the grass the cows had grazed on to produce the milk.

Now came the hardest part of the task. The curd had to be cut into small pieces with a multi-bladed curd knife, and this was back-breaking work which had to be done by a woman of ample proportions. As the vat filled with the small cubes of curd the cutting process released a liquid called whey which had to be drained from the curd through a tap at the bottom of the vat. Timing at this point was crucial, since the acids being formed affected the finished product.

By checking the acidity in the whey, the cheesemaker knew whether to speed up or delay the drainage of the liquid. Turning the curds helped to get the desired level of acidity. Once the correct level was achieved, the curds were put through a process which ground them into a mass like scrambled egg. This was sprinkled with salt to give flavour and then put into moulds. In prewar days these moulds were mostly made of elm wood and beech for strength. As the moulds were filled they were placed in presses, and when the press, which held several moulds, was full, a handle was turned to apply the required pressure. This pressure varied with the type of cheese being made, Cheshire cheese requiring much less than say, Cheddar.

In the old days all moulds were barrel shaped, but today, particularly in the cheese factories, they are more often rectangular. The cheeses were left in the presses until all surplus whey had been removed, at which point they were removed from the press and pasted with a flour and water paste before being covered with 'cheesecloth'. These days cheesecloth is more often used for polishing motor cars!

The cheeses once pasted were taken to the cheeseroom for storage. As the storage room was often upstairs, the cheesemaker had to carry the cheeses, weighing anything up to seventy pounds, up an often steep flight of stairs. They then had to be turned, end for end, daily, to ensure an even texture. Thus was made the delicious prewar cheese.

If a coloured cheese was required a vegetable dye would be added in the early stages. During the war, this dye, which came from foreign parts, was not obtainable, so instead of being its normal pinky colour, Cheshire cheese had to be a natural creamy colour, and a large proportion is like that today.

Many people, particularly the older folk, say today's cheese is not a patch on the pre-war stuff, and I agree with them. Fifty years ago it was made on the farm, matured, and came from one stock of cows.

I mustn't go on any more about cheese, but I make no apologies for my opinions for my wife was a cheesemaker on several famous Cheshire farms!

Now, how about some Cheshire Cheesemakers' tales, for as I have said, cheesemakers held a position of some importance on a farm and were able to get away with pranks that other employees could not. I have already mentioned Alice who was a cheesemaker on a large farm that was situated at the end of a long lane. This lane was the only means of access to the farm, apart from a short cut across the fields, which was only possible during the summer months, as the land was of a clay nature.

Now, for almost half a mile this lane was lined on both sides with mainly elm trees, which grew close together. It was a marvellous walk in the summer months with the sunlight filtering through the leaves and the skylarks climbing high in the heavens rendering their melodious song. In the dark dreary days of winter it was a very different scene, so dark and dreary as to seem almost frightening to the faint hearted. On a night with maybe the full moon glinting through the bare boughs, it was a daunting walk for most, even for country people. For many long years it was reputed to be a spot where ghosts appeared. The 'ladies' of the farm would not walk to the village during the dark nights, in fact some wouldn't do so even during the mellow summer evenings, unless accompanied by another person. Alice was made of sterner stuff. She pooh-poohed the idea that there might be any ghost, and would walk the lane alone even on a dark night.

This avenue was the scene of a prank that took place during the harvest and muck spreading season one year. As most local men were in full employment, it was often Irishmen who came across the water especially, when additional labour was needed at this time. Some of these men lived in a 'bothy', a building on the farm, but others lived in a part of the farmhouse, although they looked after their own needs entirely. There was one of these 'inside' men on the farm where Alice worked, a man who had been coming over from Ireland and working in the district for a number of years.

One night he had been to the hostelry in the village for his Guinness, and on getting back to the farm was asked by one of the maids if he had seen the ghost in the 'Dark Trees'. 'Ghost begorra! I'm afraid of no ghost to be sure. If there should be such an apparition I would be clouting it with me stick to be sure.' Alice heard their conversation and a night or two later, when Paddy was away for his tonic, decided to have a bit of fun. Knowing what time the pub closed and about how long Paddy would be getting to the darkest part of the lane, Alice set off with a parcel under her arm. Sure enough it wasn't long before the sound of footsteps could be heard in the distance, and Alice prepared for action. The parcel held a white dust sheet borrowed from the cleaning cupboard, and in this Alice robed herself, and hid behind a large elm.

Paddy came plodding up the lane humming an Irish melody to himself, and as soon as he passed the waiting Alice she stepped out and said in the deepest tones she could muster, 'Come here I want you.' Paddy stopped dead in his tracks, looked round, saw the sheet-clad figure, gave an almighty scream, and took to his heels, running as hard as he could for the farm and sanctuary!

Now the two maids in the farmhouse had not been aware of Alice's foray in the dark and were busy sewing by the kitchen fire, when the back door burst open and in

42

rushed an ashen-faced Paddy. The girls were of course
scared, but when they saw the mess on the floor as Paddy
made hastily for his quarters, their fright turned to dismay.
Paddy's progress could be mapped by the trail of manure
he left across the kitchen and up the stairs!

It seems that in his haste in the dark, he had taken a short
cut across the farmyard and plunged straight into the
'midden' (the pit where manure is stored). The pungent
manure was clinging to him like glue, but with each
hurried step some was dislodged, leaving an evil smelling
trail where ever he went, even up the stairs!

Alice eventually returned, using a side door, as befitted
her superior status, but it wasn't long before the maids
were calling for her in some distress, for that night the
farmer and his wife were out and had left the cheesemaker
in charge. The mess was indescribable, for by now the dog
had spread the manure in all directions. How Alice kept a
straight face will never be known, but she was a good
actress. Obviously realising she was the real cause of
the havoc, she set to and helped the maids to return the
kitchen to the spotless condition it was always in. The
smell was a bit more difficult to disperse, but by waving

lighted newspaper in the air, they got rid of all but a faint aroma which was not unusual in a farmhouse kitchen.

Now the Irishman was in a deplorable condition, smothered in the foul smelling concoction, but the next day he attributed the considerable amount of time he spent at the dolly tub to the fact that he had missed his footing when crossing the yard and found himself in the midden. There was no mention of a ghost!

A few weeks later Paddy left for his native land and was not heard of in the area again. Needless to say the legend of the ghost in the dark trees lingers on, but it was only a long while after the incident that Alice told anyone the truth of it. Alice? Although no longer a cheesemaker she's still full of fun and roars with laughter whenever she tells that story of the ghost. A sense of humour must have been most essential in those far off days when there was no television, no radio and very little money to buy reading material. Most of the fun had to be home-made, so even an incident that was far from being a laughing matter would be treated in such a way that some fun was made out of it.

In the early days of the last war many young farm workers were called up for National Service, and gradually more women and girls began to work on the farms. A certain cheesemaker had one such young girl assisting her to spring clean the dairy and cheese room. Work was well under way and there was plenty of hot water, but the supply of soda was running low. Boiling water with a little soda added (about a handful of soda to a bucket of water) was used to sterilise the various utensils in the dairy and was indispensable when woodwork, tables and the like, had to be scrubbed, for it brought the timber up a glistening white. Soda water was often used on the tables reserved for the maids' meals, too, there then being no need for a table cloth!

As the supply of soda was getting low the cheesemaker sent the young girl upstairs to fill a bucket from a bag always kept in reserve. While she was on this errand, the cheesemaker was called away and it was some time before she was able to return to the scene of operations, where the young girl was still busy scrubbing. As the job was nearing completion the cheesemaker replaced the various items in their allotted positions, thinking as she did so that the new girl had made a good job of them, for there appeared to be a shine on the metal that was not normally present. The job was completed and nothing thought of it until the next day, although the farmer, on passing through the dairy, did remark, 'This yer floor be a bit on the slidy side.'

The next day the farmer's wife was cooking, for most of the cooking was done by the lady of the house, when she found she was short of sugar. Calling the maid who had the previous day helped in the dairy, she sent her to the room upstairs for a basin of sugar. Soon the maid returned and handed the 'missus' the basin. Straight away she could see that it was soda the girl had brought, not sugar. 'Ye girt numkin,' she said, 'Don't 'ee know t'difference of sugar from soda?' 'Well', said the maid, 'I used some of that stuff out of t'other basin to scrub t'dairy with yesterday.' 'Tha daft wench' said the farmer's wife, 'boss'll go mad, with this ere scrapping (war) on, sweetning be scarce'.

Of course the farmer's wife had to investigate in the dairy and found that everything that had been scrubbed had a nice gloss which was in fact a very thin coating of sugar that had set hard! Not being at all amused at the waste of almost unobtainable sugar, she had to tell the farmer when he came in, maybe hoping that either the cheese-maker or the maid would get a scolding. However the farmer was a humorous man and merely said, 'Well Missus, we'm a bit down on sugar, so we'll go without any in our tea for a week'. There were protests but he insisted, adding, 'I'll be seeing old so-and-so soon, he wants a ham, so we can do a swop.'

Of course in country districts even during the leanest years of the war, there were not many shortages for there was always something to barter for what you needed; a ham for sugar for instance. This practice often extended beyond the farming community, for local shopkeepers usually had something 'under the counter' and many a swop took place when the local bobby was known to be off duty!

The Womens' Land Army was formed during the war years, and many of the women who worked on the farms were quick to join, for a uniform was issued and this was a great saving on the clothing coupons of those days. Also the employer had to pay a fixed wage to women in the Land Army, and in many cases this was quite a bit more than most farmers were paying. Many town girls were directed to work on the land, for home food production was an essential part of war-time economy. Most adapted to rural life pretty well, some of course hated it, and a few married village lads and still live in rural areas.

Of course the farmer's wife directed the day-to-day work within the house, but should additional help be needed on the land such as during the hay harvest, the farmer soon had the girls in the fields. As a rule the lady of the house spent most of her time within those confines, at least during the day, but in the evening she would often set off with her husband by horse and trap and later by car (farmers started getting motor transport in the mid 1930s) to visit other farmers for a card evening, whist probably being the favourite game. Their games would often go on into the early hours, for they always partook of a feed. There would also be home-made wine, for country folk of all classes made use of many fruits and flowers to produce often potent drinks.

On one occasion a farmer had been to one of these card parties, leaving his wife at home, for she was indisposed. In the early hours he came home, or rather the pony brought him home, and as he bumped into various things on his way to the stairs he naturally disturbed his wife. When he eventually reached the stairs and then slipped down a tread, she woke with a jolt. 'That you John?' she called 'Aye Missus' he said. 'What you making so much noise for?' was the reply. 'I'm trying to get these bottles of wine upstairs, that owd Tom gave me.' 'Dunna bother with them tonight', she said, but John shouted back, 'I'll 'avta, I've supped 'em'. No doubt there would be 'tongue sauce' for breakfast the next morning.

Many wives received very little in the way of cash from their farmer husbands, and so had to get their pin money in various ways. There would be a flock of hens roaming the farmyard, real free-range birds, and the eggs produced were taken or sent to market, the proceeds going into the lady of the house's pocket. Some would make a few pounds of butter, which was often sold at the door. Christmas would be a busy time where the lady had reared a few turkeys or maybe geese. These were always sold plucked and dressed, or as they say today, oven-ready. If there were a large number of birds to be dealt with, the farm-workers' wives would be called in to assist between the milking sessions. The timing of this job was pretty important, there being no refrigerators or cold rooms for the dressed birds to be stored in, and should the weather be mild, as it often is before Christmas, the preparation of the birds had to be delayed for as long as possible. Poultry will soon 'go off' in humid conditions so it was often very close to the twenty fifth before the task began.

One such year, when the weather had been almost spring-like a week before Christmas, no birds had been dressed. Then three days before, the weather changed, with a biting east wind and snow in the air. I had to call at a farmhouse one evening, and there were three women in the kitchen, with a roaring fire, busy getting the 'jackets' (feathers) off the turkeys. Fluff and feathers were everywhere! I asked why they weren't in the usual outhouse and was told that it was much too cold, and numb fingers couldn't pull feathers. As it was Christmas time the lady of the house offered me a bottle of beer, and proceeded to pour it out into a glass. In a matter of moments the froth on the beer was covered in fluff and small feathers. Politeness made me drink it after unobtrusively getting rid of the froth and fluff.

After a while I remarked on the vast number of feathers drifting in the air, all gradually settling on the furniture or slowly going up the chimney. Liz, the farmer's wife said, 'It's nowt lad. We'll get the hose and "weldon" (yard) brush in, when us as finished.' I could imagine it would take almost as long to clear the mess up as it took to dress the turkeys. All the farmers' wives were good hardworking women, mostly generous and caring and often pillars of the local community, taking an active part in most aspects of village life, the Womens' Institute, the Mothers' Union, and various other organisations.

4 *The woodland scene*

The previous three chapters have covered in some small way the farmlands and those who worked thereon, but woodlands are also to be found in most areas of the country. Some of course are owned by farmers, but the majority of timber growing areas tend to be found on the large estates, that is if you do not count the woodlands of the Forestry Commission.

Today, even these estates plant a vast number of softwood trees; larch, spruce, and so on, but in the past much of the timber was grown for use on the estates, and consisted of a pretty wide range of trees from oak, through the hardwoods to spruce, larch and poplar. Each type of timber had its use and therefore woodlands were well cared for, the end product being so important.

Planting trees is a long term project, carried out with the next generation in mind. In many cases one generation of foresters followed another, handing down from father to son, and perhaps to grandson a vast understanding of the ways of the woods, and an immense skill in the use of the necessary tools. For in those days, there was no recourse to the petrol saw, tractor and crane, or for that matter to the sprays now used to control unwanted growth round newly planted saplings.

It was all either hand or horse work, although of course it was done at a much more leisurely pace and I am sure in many, even most cases, to a higher standard. A number of years would pass before a lad starting at the age of fourteen, became capable of using all the tools needed in the course of a year's work. Normally the lad's job during his first year with a gang of woodmen was that of 'can lad'. This involved lighting a fire and keeping it in good shape throughout the day, summer or winter, for his main task was to brew the tea. No flasks for the working man. Starting at six in the morning, or around seven o'clock during the winter months, he had to have a nice clear fire going, and cans, sometimes eight or nine of them, boiling rapidly in time to make the mash for eight o'clock breakfast.

Each woodman would have his own can, a special tea can, for this purpose. After it had boiled around a wood fire a few times, it looked the same as all the others, but the lad had to know the owner of each, for he would be in trouble if he gave an old-timer the wrong can. Blackened by the smoke and flames one would wonder how a good drink of tea could be made in the can, but there was a trick to stop the water getting smoked. As soon as the water started to boil, a small piece of wood was placed in the can, usually a dead piece trimmed of bark. This stopped the water getting smoke-tainted, though I have never been able to fathom out how. Nevertheless, before the 'twist' of tea was put into the boiling water a small amount was poured off, if only to make room for the milk.

The water was no problem: the cans would be taken to the nearest source, be it river, pond or brook. Boiling no doubt rendered it harmless, and somehow it seemed to impart a special taste to the tea, which was always drunk from the can lid!

Whilst the woodmen were having their break they would often sharpen their tools, axes, hooks and the like, and thus the lad would start to learn how the tools of the

49

trade should be looked after, and of course, now and again, he was left a tool not in use to practise with. It was essential that all cutting edges should be kept sharp since this made the inevitable heavy work that much lighter.

At the end of the day, five o'clock in the evening in the summer, and when the first pheasant went to roost in the winter, each woodman would gather his tools and move some distance away and hide them. One old lad always said as he was covering his with leaves, 'I con see ye, dinna be a' comin' back later', a ritual with him, although who knows, he might have had some of this tools stolen in the past.

Tree falling or felling was an important part of a woodman's job but not necessarily the most important. It may be the harvest, but there is also the 'sowing' to be done, and there is a correct time for that too. Sandy Myles, one time head forester (the head man was always called 'forester', but the men who worked in the woods, 'woodmen',) used to say when talking about planting young trees, 'Plant 'em in November and you can tell 'em to grow, plant 'em in February and you've got to ask 'em'. He was talking mainly about hardwoods, for March and April are probably the best months for the softwood seedling to be planted.

If an area of wood had been clean felled, that is, all timber removed, and was going to be replanted, Sandy would visit the site and stick up several thin poles. This would indicate the direction in which he wished the line of seedlings to be planted, and there would also be a stick or two to show how far apart the two foot high young trees should be. It was normal in those days to plant quite large plants, as one woodman said, 'So its yed be above the rubbish'. By this he meant: so that the leader would be clear of the growth of summer weeds.

When the waggoners had delivered the supply of young trees the woodmen would arrive and start planting, working in pairs. It was amazing how large an area they could cover in a day. One would use a sharp spade and the other carry a bundle of plants. The man with the spade made a triangular cut in the soil, then pushing the spade down to its limit, prised the soil up and his mate pushed the plant into the cut. The full weight of the planter was then placed over the cut and the plant made firm in the ground.

The men worked entirely by eye, lining up on the poles placed by Sandy, and it wasn't long before a row as straight as a die reached from one end of the planting area to the other. The head forester, during some stage of the planting operation, was sure to arrive to inspect progress, and he would catch hold of some of the young trees, and give them a sharp tug, to see if they were firmly in the ground. Woe betide anyone who was responsible for a plant that gave way to Sandy's pull!

Some of the woods I remember being planted are a living monument to those old timers and a pleasure to behold. No large stands of uninteresting softwoods, but an area of mixed hardwoods, with considerable under-growth to host all the indigenous wildlife.

The summer following the original planting the gang of woodmen came back to 'clean' the young trees. This was done with a short-bladed scythe, sometimes called a briar scythe, which was ideal for cutting the unwanted summer growth from around the newly planted trees. It was a task that was always left until at least mid-summer, for any game birds had to be left undisturbed to rear their brood, and of course there would be numerous migratory warblers nesting in the ideal conditions.

There was much more respect for wildlife in general in those distant days, and most of the men had an intimate knowledge and great interest in the inhabitants of the woods, so much of the work was done during the winter months. Today, trees are felled in full leaf and then kiln dried, but the end product is not a patch on naturally matured wood.

Not a tree would be felled until all the leaves had fallen, which was usually in November, and then enough selected trees would be taken from the mature woods to meet the estimated needs of the estate in three years' time, a pretty constant amount in fact, but it took three years to mature.

The skill required to fall one huge tree amongst many others was vast, but a good woodman could fall any tree, more or less in any spot, for it was essential that no un-

necessary damage was caused to any younger trees, the crop of the future. It was all done by hand of course and was hard work too. Two men were needed and both had to be skilled. The first job was to assess the height of the tree and which side carried the most weight, the largest boughs. Then it had to be decided which was the best direction in which to 'drop' the tree. Once these often difficult decisions had been made a 'face' would have to be cut at the base of the trunk and all spurs going into the ground trimmed. The cutting of the face decided which way the fall would be, and the removal of the 'spurs' ensured there would be no twisting action.

Axes as sharp as razors were used to put the 'face' on the trunk, and to see two men swinging these six or seven pound tools was a sight never to be forgotten. With alternate strokes the chips of wood would fly until a sloping face was achieved. Sometimes, on a very large tree, the face would start three or more feet from the ground and be more than a foot into the trunk at the base, which required a lot of axe work.

Once a satisfactory 'face' had been cut the sawing would begin. The men would use a huge cross-cut saw, sometimes six or seven feet in length with many shark's teeth to do the cutting. When the saw was bedded in the trunk and the men were in rhythm with their work, the sawdust soon mounted. The cut was always made at ground level, and the men would be on their knees pulling in turn on the huge saw. Pulling is the operative word for no matter how slowly his partner pulled the saw to him, it was useless for the other chap to try and push, for the saw would tend to bend and pulling it became that much more difficult.

Eventually the tree would topple and come to the ground with an almighty crash. Sometimes one of the woodmen would grab an axe and give one or two sharp blows to the edge of the face. This was done when it looked as if the tree would not fall quite where required. Skilful and nimble men those old foresters were.

Once the tree was down it had to be trimmed up, and most of this work was done with the axe. Maybe an extra large limb would be cut through with a saw, but very little of the tree would be wasted. Once the limbs had been cut off, they would be cut into more or less uniform lengths and stacked. This 'cordwood', as it was called, would be carted later to the sawbench, the best of it being eventually cut into stakes, and the rest turned into logs. The remainder, 'brash' as it was called, was burnt on the spot and this task often fell to the lad who had been working for twelve months or so. A small fire was started, using slithers of bark from a birch tree, if these were available, or with a handful of dry grass and very fine twigs; rarely indeed did a good lad need any paper to get a fire going. Gradually the fire would be built up by adding larger and larger pieces of bark, but each piece had to be cut to a reasonable length, four feet or so, and laid on the fire in a certain way, not thrown on anyhow.

The lad would now be learning to use the tools of the trade. Holding these smaller boughs in one hand and putting the end of some across the fire, he would cut them with a billhook. The material to be burnt was always placed across the direction of the wind. After a quantity had been burnt, there would be a pause in feeding the flames until the centre had been burnt out of the fire. Then, using a 'pikel', the ends remaining on either side would be placed on the glowing embers where they would burst almost immediately into flames. Then the process would be repeated until all the 'brash' was disposed of.

Not only would the tree have been cut down at ground level, and the trunk and brash dealt with in a proper manner, but it was the custom to rake all the twigs and chipping onto the embers of the fire, and thus in a matter of weeks, when the spring growth started, it was difficult to see where a giant of the wood had once stood.

When a number of trees in a wood had been thus treated, the waggoners, with their timber carriages would arrive to take the trunks to the sawyard. These men were expert at putting what was very often an awkward load onto the special carriage. Often by using 'skids' and chains the two horses would pull a massive tree trunk into position. In some cases a 'three legs' had to be used, although always with the same result: a well balanced load.

After the trees had been cut and carried to the sawmill, it would be some considerable time before a saw was used on them. When this did happen the trunk would be 'slabbed', that is cut from the base to the top of the trunk, and then stacked with thin laths of wood between each slab so that the air could circulate and season the timber. When slabbed and restacked with the laths between, the tree would appear to be a larger version of the original, due to the air spaces. After twelve months or so, the timber thus treated would be naturally seasoned, and was suitable for many jobs on the estate.

Eventually, after maybe three or four years, the slabs would be cut down to whatever size was needed for gate-posts, fencing posts, rails and stakes, and the better quality slabs would be made into gates and many other items. Timber treated in this natural way will last for many many years. Quite recently I was talking about these matters to an old lad well into his eighties, and I happened to ask how long well-treated timber lasted. He told me about a post-and-rail fence that was still sound and commented, 'We did that thar, the year "Tipperary Tim" won the National', (the mid 1920s). Sheer curiosity made me go and look at it, and sure enough apart from one or two posts with the shakes it was still in pretty good condition.

The same old chap told me that if you really want a fence to last, you should use split oak, that is lengths of the timber split with an axe, and for that matter, cut to length with an axe also. It appears, and on reflection this is only common sense, that cutting wood with a saw opens up the grain and lets the water in, causing early rotting, whereas splitting follows the grain, and water is less able to penetrate the wood. There are a few fences made by this splitting method still around, and I know a short length, where the posts, rails and pales, (it was a paling fence) are still sound although it was probably put up at the turn of the century, and it's much the same as it was fifty five years ago!

The scythe was a tool of great importance in those days. It dates back many centuries, but no one could wield it better than an experienced woodman. It is a really individual tool, for men of different height or stance cannot use the same implement to the best advantage. If a man needed a new blade it had to be fixed to the 'pow' (handle) by the blacksmith, for heat was needed to set the blade at the correct angle to suit the man using it. Much care was taken over this, for it meant the difference between hard or reasonably easy work, and a good or bad job.

The 'edge' on a scythe is of course most important, and most of those old woodmen would stop work and 'tickle 'er up' every few yards according to the herbage being cut. A 'whetstone' was used for this, a coarse round stone about a foot long and about two inches in diameter at the centre, tapered down to an inch or so. The coarseness of the stone gave a rather rough edge to the blade, which helped its cutting action.

During the summer months much work had to be done with a scythe: trimming round young trees, cutting openings in the woods and cutting the tracks or rides which were the ways through the wooded areas. On one occasion I went to see a gang of woodmen cutting tracks through a wood with many drainage ditches. The first woodman who came into sight was leaning on a handrail that was attached to a plank crossing one such ditch. After a short conversation Neddy Taylor, the woodman, shouted 'Ow', threw his scythe in the air (it landed in the water filled ditch) and departed along the track at great speed! Then a pair of trousers were seen to fly into the air amid shouts of 'Oh! Ouch!' and not a little foul language. Neddy had been standing on a wasps' nest, and many of them had found their way up his trousers legs! Despite the fact that it was hot weather Neddy was wearing long Johns and maybe it was as well, for untold damage might have been done without them.

It was a sight never to be forgotten for Neddy was only about five feet five and almost as much in girth, and he looked a bit like a barrel as he rushed noisily along the track. It was a long while before he returned to retrieve his scythe and it was most noticeable the next day, that whilst mowing tracks, his trousers were tied round his ankles!

The estate with which I am most familiar has a number

of drives leading from main roads to the big house. As was the custom in those days, each drive entrance had a lodge. The lodge-keepers were in the main, ex-servicemen from the First World War, two of whom had lost an arm, so were to a degree handicapped. However, the entrances to the estate had to be kept in a tidy and presentable condition and the woodmen had to do the heavier work. Most lodges had quite large lawns, or should I say patches of grass, both inside and outside the gates. This of course had to be mowed in the summer and it was an impossible task for a one-armed man to use a scythe, so the skill of the woodmen came to the fore. Every Saturday morning rain or shine, for weather did not deter the old timers, a couple of woodmen would arrive at the lodge with one of the apprentices and start to mow the grass. Now the grass would only be a couple of inches long at most, and anyone who has tried to cut grass with a scythe will know how difficult a heavy crop is to deal with, let alone a light one.

Bill Salisbury, Arthur 'Top' Jones, Jack Thomas and Watty Huxley could deal with that short crop all right. The main thing of course was that the scythe should be set right, with an edge like a razor. With pendulum swings these men would proceed across a lawn, and in a short while have the job completed. When the light crop had been raked off by the lad leaving a surface almost like a billiard table, it was impossible to see any of the 'swing' marks. The edges were cut with the same implement, and it is safe to say that the final effect was way ahead of anything that can be achieved by the modern hover or rotary machine.

There were of course machines in those days, a number being in use in the pleasure gardens, but it was impracticable to cart these around the lodges. In fact with many horses about, a quantity of flints and chippings would be in the grass, and while they wouldn't do the cylinder of an expensive mowing machine much good, unless they were extremely large, they would not have a great impact on the edge of a scythe.

There were, in fact still are, several types of scythe, varying in a number of ways, and to a certain extent each was designed for a specific job. Some had short blades, like briar scythes, some had long thin blades like the old corn cutting implement; some had a lot of bend in the blade, some very little. By and large the expert would stick to his favourite style, with maybe two types of blade, depending on the type of cutting to be done, and under no circumstances would he allow anyone either to sharpen or use his scythe.

Some had a particular choice of 'pow' (handle) or 'stail'. These had varying degrees of bend or 'come' in them, though they were almost straight. No matter its style or combination of styles each tool had to be fitted to the user, and when the combination was right, mowing by an experienced man looked so easy. Shuffling one foot in front of the other with each swing of the blade he made it seem effortless.

It must however have been an effort to mow an acre a day as one old lad told me he had done, years ago, and that was of corn!

Two 'can lads' were once trimming saplings into walking sticks as lads will do, when one cut his finger rather badly. All the woodmen were busy but the other lad bound the damaged finger with a piece of rag, and then proceeded to admonish him, telling him how he ought to use not just a knife, but any cutting tool: 'Cut away from you Bill, how many times do you want telling. You don't see Watty using a knife like you were, perhaps you have learnt your lesson though.' When the gang of men returned to the fire, they of course wanted to know what had happened and John explained that he had told Bill always to cut away from himself. 'Aye that be good advice, but 'taint always true, when you'm using a scythe, the'e cuts round thisself'. Of course there are other occasions when that advice is not quite accurate, such as when using a spokeshave, an adze or maybe even cutting a slice of bread. But in general, at least as far as a knife is concerned, 'cut away' is a sound rule.

Most of a woodman's work was concerned with the maintenance of the wooded areas on an estate, but at the same time many of the jobs involved providing for the needs of the big house. As has been mentioned, the larger boughs which could not be used for posts, stakes, or even smaller hedging stakes, were carted to the sawbench, as

57

the saw mill was called, and there in due course they were cut into logs. Now of course all timber will burn, but some types burn better than others. Most country folk had a preference for a particular timber be it ash, beech, oak or elm, but the big house was normally supplied with large quantities of ash or beech. Now things were so organised that timber cut one year was logged the next winter, and probably not used on the vast open fires at the house until a year after that. These logs were well seasoned and dry, and would throw off a terrific heat, this being essential in the very large rooms. Most of the hardwoods burnt reasonably slowly, but as a rule, ash and beech give a brighter fire than the rather slower burning oak.

The various elms were never used at the big house, but logs made from this timber found their way onto the cottagers' fires, many of whom had a load of logs at Christmas. White and wych elm would split quite well, especially soon after felling, but black elm was never very popular, for once it started to dry out it was almost impossible for a man to drive an axe into it. Even by using wedges and a seven pound hammer it could only be broken down into a suitable size with very great difficulty. There was an old saying: 'Black elm will warm you more than any other, once when splitting and once again when burning'. The only snag here was that unless the wood was just about on the point of going rotten, it didn't burn very well either.

Softwoods, the various spruces, larch and Scotch pine, were rarely used for logs. As soon as they start to burn they tend to throw off a lot of sparks, and are thus considered a fire hazard. A knotty piece of Scotch pine, was not quite so bad, and being often full of resin, would give off a terrific heat.

Much of the softwood grown went for pit props, especially the thinnings, that is timber cut when comparatively young. Mature softwoods, trees between forty and fifty years old, could be seasoned for use mainly in the building trade. Now all these logs that were delivered to the big house needed something to start them off, and of course there were many coal fires as well that needed 'starting sticks' or what is probably better known as kindling wood. For this purpose, small twigs and branches previously gathered in bundles called 'faggots', were chopped to the required length.

Certain areas of woodland were set aside to produce these faggots and for other purposes. In some parts of the country this is called 'coppicing', but the word seems to be applied more where hazel and maybe young ash are the main growth. In Cheshire hazel does not grow in great abundance, but many woods have plenty of young sycamore growing beneath the older trees. Now sycamore ignites easily when it is seasoned and dry, and it was therefore the main component of those prewar faggots.

Each area used to produce faggots, would be cropped around every seven years, so really seven areas were needed, each being cut once in that period. They had to be fairly large areas for maybe upwards of two hundred and fifty of these bundles would be needed to provide an adequate supply.

None of the 'coppicing' work was done until late November or December, when all the leaves had fallen and there was very little sap in the wood. The woodmen who did the work were skilled men. It may not appear to take much skill to cut down young undergrowth which is a maximum of about two inches in diameter, but it had to be cut in such a way that another crop could be taken in seven or so years' time, and so that some of the material cut could be sorted for uses other than faggots.

As usual the essential thing was a sharp implement, and the billhook was the tool used. Before work began it was necessary to obtain a bundle of 'red withen' per man, this being used to tie the bundles of faggots and other wood. The red withen was most suitable for this, as it makes a growth of four feet or so a year, and remains pliable throughout the winter.

Each woodmen would obtain a bundle of these withen, which seemed to be grown for this particular job, and before cutting the saplings, would make them into what were known as bands. A rather apt name, for when fastened firmly round the bundle of thin wood (faggot) the bright reddish-purple of the band showed up like a painted strip on the green sycamore. It was not easy to make the withen bands, but by a twirl of the cut withen, held at the thin end, and a deft twist, and doubling back of the thinnest part, a loop was formed.

Once the woodman started to cut the young sycamore growth for faggots he would reduce each piece to yard lengths. When the bundle had reached the required size the woodman would slip a band round it, put the thicker end through the loop, tread on the bundle, and with a twisting action whilst holding the band, fasten the whole lot together. These bundles of faggots were often left for a while to season a little before being carted to the 'stick house' to be stacked for use at a later date.

The 'stick house' was a covered building with open sides to allow a free flow of air, and here the faggots were eventually cut into suitable lengths for fire kindling. An older man had this task throughout the winter months, it was a full time job too, chopping kindling sticks and splitting logs which were needed in large quantities.

Now not all the material cut was used for faggots. If a piece of sycamore or ash should be fairly straight and of the right dimensions it would be trimmed – all the trimmings going into the faggots – cut to the right length and laid aside. When a dozen similar pieces had accumulated, they would be tied in the same fashion as the faggots but using two bands, and set aside for use as bean sticks or poles, which of course were in great demand in the spring to grow runner beans on.

Any bushy growth in the area being cleared would also be bundled up and eventually used as pea sticks. Neither sycamore nor ash provided much in the way of pea sticks, but often there were old 'seats' of elm trees in the area, and many of these would produce a lot of growth which was most suitable for pea sticks. Now these pea sticks, when cut, were laid out in small heaps and the bundles of bean sticks were laid across them, in order to flatten the bushy pea sticks, and make them much easier to handle when staking the rows of peas. These heaps of bean and pea sticks would often be left in the woods until spring, when they would be collected and taken to the kitchen gardens or wherever needed.

The red willow (withen) used as bands to tie the various

products of coppicing differs from the willow used for basket making which is white. Both varieties grow well in damp and boggy places, but the white willow makes for the sky (grows straight up) and the red flops over and layers itself in the boggy soil.

Many estates in the old days would utilize any otherwise useless piece of boggy land prone to flooding, to grow a crop of willow for basket making. The willow wands would simply be pushed into the soft earth, the top cut off, and in a few years a saleable crop of willow would be produced.

Unlike the undergrowth cut for faggots and so on, which needed a seven year growth, willows had to be cut each and every year, for they made such rapid growth that most two year old willows were in little demand. Some larger wands were always needed for the larger and stronger basket work, but as a rule there would be a fair proportion of one year growth that would meet this demand.

Now timber felling, at least in prewar days, took place during the winter months when the sap was down, but there were different requirements when it came to willow. It was necessary for there to be a certain amount of sap in the willows when they were cut, for this facilitated the stripping of the bark. As willow grew in moist and often waterlogged places, during the summer months it drew a vast amount of water up into the stems. This was essential to their tremendous growth, but if the willow wands were cut during the height of the growing season, once they were seasoned there was a tendency for them to be brittle.

Autumn or early spring, October or March maybe, were the normal cutting times for the white willow for basket making, for at these times there was just the right amount of sap in the stems for that purpose. The woodmen were experts at harvesting the willow, and here, as in all rural jobs, quite a lot of skill was required. Special knives were used, of a most unusual shape, being very curved and having what appeared at first glance to be a piece cut out of the most curved part of the blade. This gap was the most important part of the knife and was in fact the cutting edge. In this case, the operator did cut towards himself, for he placed this sharp gap in the curved blade round the base of

61

the withen to be cut, and held the withen in the other hand. A sharp pull upwards and towards himself resulted in a clean cut. As the withens were cut and usually graded at the same time, they were placed in bundles and then tied with a couple of bands in the same manner as the bean sticks.

Often the lads tied the cut willow and carried it to a central point, whilst the older men trimmed what were in effect the 'pollarded' willow. If there was a dead stump of willow in the long lines, a suitable piece would be inserted to take its place, and the dead stump was removed and burnt by the can lads.

Once the whole bed had been cropped, horses and carts would arrive to collect the bundles and deliver them to the local basket maker. His yard might well have been some distance away, so carts were preferable to lorries, for a hundred or so bundles of cut withen would be of considerable weight and were not particularly good things to load. In many cases the same craftsman would buy the crop of willow year after year. Sadly many old willow beds are no longer cropped, and it seems that imported baskets have killed the demand for the English made article and with it the skill of cutting the wands, which is a shame.

The men often had fun during their arduous tasks in the woods, and one small incident comes to mind, in fact it happened almost every withen cutting for a number of years. Watty Huxley, one of the woodmen, was a great man for a bit of fun. He was a very good athlete, and took part in local sports regularly. The long jump was his speciality and he was seldom beaten in this event. Now in one particular willow bed, there was a main watercourse, in fact quite a wide brook. This brook meandered through the water meadows, and on through the willows. At lunch times when the men and lads sat round the fire eating their 'bagging', it was inevitable that someone would bring up sport and this always led on to Watty's ability to jump the brook. The talk of sport was deliberate, for almost every year there would be a new lad or two in the gang, and everyone but the unsuspecting new recruits, knew what was coming.

Watty always egged them on until almost without fail one of the lads, would say, 'I bet I can jump as far as you Mr Huxley', (note the 'Mr' Huxley, no christian name terms in those days). Well it was quite understandable for Watty was not a very big man, had a tendency to be bow-legged and did not give the impression of great agility. How deceiving that impression was!

Now Watty would say, 'Do you reckon as you could jump the brook?' The lad would say, 'If you can, I can,' and thus the trap was set. Watty would say 'Right ye pick the spot and I'll go first'. With some deliberation the lad would find a place with a good run up and a good take off point, which didn't really bother Watty too much. Casting his jacket aside but still wearing his heavy hob-nailed boots Watty would run at the brook bank, take one tremendous leap and land on the other side. 'Come on lad, let's see 'ee do it'. Of course the lad would run at the brook bank at a tremendous pace, and then the inevitable happened, he landed in the middle of the brook! On one such occasion a lad didn't get that far even, he tripped as he reached the brook bank and landed flat on his face in the water! Fortunately the brook was not in flood, the water being only quite shallow, but the unfortunate lad had to spend much of the afternoon around the fire drying out. They never seemed to suffer any ill effects from these soakings, perhaps being a tougher breed than today.

63

I mustn't forget to say that the brook was quite wide, they say eighteen feet. I have not measured the distance, but I certainly would not have attempted it, not even in my youth!

5 *The woodman's skills*

The previous chapter dealt mainly with the woodmens'
work, but did not describe in any detail some of the
specialist jobs requiring great skill and dedication which
were carried out by these men. Most woodmen could
tackle most of the jobs in the woods, but there were always
jobs to be done beyond the confines of the wood.

Now fencing is essential in the countryside, for despite
the great care taken of hedges, there are always some
positions in which the thorn will not grow well enough
to make an impenetrable hedge. A typical place would
be around a wood. There was probably a good sound
hawthorn hedge at one time, for in the old days when a
wood was planted a thorn hedge was required as a
perimeter fence. With the passing of time, as the trees
grew, many of them would overhang the hedge, and
eventually the canopy would slowly kill the hedge. It
would have been useless to plant thorn 'quicks' in such
gaps, so the alternative was post-and-rail fencing. Today, as
a matter of economy one must suppose, an odd stake and a

strand or two of that bane of the countryside, barbed wire, is more likely to be used.

None of the woodmen, who were nearly all country men, would have cared to use barbed wire in prewar days. 'What about the hunt' would be the cry, for barbed wire, horses and hounds do not go well together. Estate owners would not normally allow this miserable 'breeches tearer' to be used, but as the years passed it came into greater use, maybe because the tenant farmers could no longer get a supply of free posts, stakes and rails from the estate. This had been the custom for many years, but the Second World War changed many things, among them, the free supply of fencing material from the estate sawyard.

Stakes, posts and rails came in all lengths and sizes, and were of well seasoned timber, which, after sawing had been in the pickling tank for a week. This tank held a lot of material, and creosote was pumped into it under pressure for the whole period. When the seasoned timber was removed the creosote had penetrated right through it. Much of that prewar pickled fencing is still around and serving a useful purpose today.

There is naturally another reason why there is still some serving its original purpose, and that is the skill of the men who erected it! It was not a hit or miss job. First the length to be fenced would be cleared of all debris and the line of the fence decided on. The rails were laid out in matching pairs, length-wise that is, or in threes if it was to be a three rail fence. At the ends of the rails a post would be laid and in between a stake. Once the material was in position, the erecting would commence.

Posts were always dug in, and a 'grafting' spade used to excavate a hole large and deep enough for the piece of creosoted timber which usually measured six inches by four inches. When the hole was of the correct depth it would be placed in position and the soil gradually 'punned' around it. A 'punner' was often made out of a suitable piece of rail. The rail was shaved off at one end and the other left square, and by using this implement with quite a bit of force the soil would be firmed round the post until it became impossible to move it.

The rail would then be placed against the first post, and

at the correct distance another hole excavated for the next post. With two posts in position, a rail would be nailed to the top, giving the line the fence was going to take. No matter how hard the ground might be it was considered bad workmanship to cut anything off the post just to save moving more soil!

The stake which was to go mid-way between the two posts was always driven in with a sledge hammer, for being of smaller dimensions it would have been difficult to secure it if a hole had been dug. The men who did the fencing had driving in those stakes down to a fine art, but one old lad, Harry Roberts, nearly slipped up one day. They were getting on fine with a particular length of fence, and there were no problems until almost the last stake, which could not be driven in straight, probably because of a large stone below the surface. Harry kept stopping the chap wielding the sledge hammer and making adjustments to the position of the stake, and eventually thought he had it just right. The sledge hammer came down with a thump, and still the stake was not going in to Harry's satisfaction. More minor adjustments, and by now the chap wielding the seven pound hammer was getting frustrated. He said, 'Come on Harry, we'll be all week.' This comment was ignored for a while and then Harry said, 'When I nod my head you 'it it!' A good job the striker didn't take poor old Harry literally, since a blow on the head with a seven pound hammer would have needed some explaining!

Various types of fencing were erected, depending on what was required at a particular spot. The normal fence round a wood would be made of posts, stakes and two parallel rails, the rails being between twelve and fifteen inches apart, and then midway between the bottom rail and the ground a length of fencing wire would be run. The wire had to be stretched taut and this required a special device, a 'wire strainer' which was often made by the local blacksmith, usually out of scrap material. One end of the wire would be securely fastened to the end post, run out the full length of the fence, and then stapled at the correct height. None of these staples would be driven home, except when the wire had been 'strained', and then only on the last post. If it was an exceptionally long length of fence, the staples would be driven home about every fifty yards, for that was about the limit at which the 'strainer' would operate efficiently. It was considered bad workmanship to drive the staples home, for one thing it made it very difficult to remove the wire should it be necessary.

Fields that were used to graze horses regularly would need a four-feet-high fence as opposed to the normal three-feet plus and always consisted of posts, stakes and four rows of rails. Another fence might consist of a single rail, and three or even four strands of wire, depending on what was likely to be grazing the field.

Never was a line or level used, all was done by eye, and over often uneven ground the fencing was a credit to the skill of those old time woodmen. The head forester was very particular and it was not unknown for a length to have to be redone simply because a stake was just a fraction out of line! The numerous 'hunting hatches' (small gates in most of the boundary hedges) were dealt with by another department of the estate.

Alongside the fences and hedges there were often ditches and main water-courses, which all needed regular attention. A gang of men would spend most of the year keeping the many miles of water courses in good condition and good working order. The tenant farmers were responsible for the ditches on their farms but where main watercourses and brooks were concerned, the estate 'brookers' came in. Today the Water Board do the main brooks, using either a dredger or a J.C.B. leaving many smaller lengths untouched, but in the old days there was normally a gang of three brookers. Those old lads had a hard task, first cutting the annual growth of herbage with a scythe, then the overhanging branches with a hook, then raking all the debris up the bank, before getting into the water and using a spade to remove any soil that had fallen in or might have been trodden in by cattle.

They had no rubber boots or waders, just heavy leather boots up to the knee, and thick hessian sacks tied round the waist like aprons. It doesn't need much imagination to visualize the scene: three chaps in a wide ditch shovelling wet sloppy mud onto the bank, splashing mud everywhere, their hands and faces covered in it.

I remember I stood and watched when the brookers were working gaily away. One of them was smoking his pipe, the smoke curling high into the still air. Seeing him smoking made me get my pipe and baccy out, and as I proceeded to fill the bowl, I looked up, and immediately roared with laughter. The men stopped working at once, and one said, 'I can't see nowt to laugh at lad.' Well he couldn't, but as I had filled my pipe, I looked at the face carved on the bowl, (carved pipes were in vogue at the time) and side ways on it was a perfect copy of one of the brookers' faces. All I got for my sense of humour was a shovel full of sloppy mud thrown at me which I neatly dodged. I have still got that pipe fifty years on, but Isaac departed this earth many years ago.

As they worked their way along a watercourse, normally working upstream, against the flow, they would inspect and clear any field drains that emptied into the brook, and sometimes even remove one or two of the end earthen-ware drains to clear an obstruction.

An eel was sometimes thrown on to the bank with a shovel of slurry, and there would be a mad dive to capture it before it slithered back into the water. Many a country person was fond of eels but how anyone could eat one coming out of that thick glutinous muck I do not know. Whilst on the subject of eels, the brookers were once repairing a field drain on the edge of a stream, and before putting the three-inch pipes back, one old lad poked a stick up and to his surprise, found that something soft was preventing it from entering very far. The other men had a go with no better luck and after some discussion they decided that there was only one thing for it, they would have to remove another pipe or so. It was quite a deep drain, so the task was not approached with much relish, but when after some time a couple of the foot-long pipes had been taken out, the soft object could be seen – an eel! Now these old lads were not much given to exaggeration, but they all swore that it filled the three-inch pipe. It must have been some eel, but as its weight never seems to have been mentioned, perhaps the actual size should be taken with a pinch of salt! Eels will use field drains to get from a watercourse to a pond, and even when there is a heavy morning dew, they cross overland, but it is doubtful if any large enough to get stuck in a drain make such a journey.

A river running through the countryside is normally the responsibility of an Authority of some sort, in the old days it was a river board, now a Water Authority. These river boards employed men to maintain the flow of the river, and prevent or repair bank erosion. All the heavy and sometimes dangerous work was done by hand and required great skill. Often, after the winter floods, a large tree would be hanging dangerously over the water, with many of its roots exposed. It was no easy task to cut it down and get it onto the bank. If it was at all possible it would be done with the use of a winch. One of the men would climb the tree and secure a wire rope at a selected place, often almost at the top of the tree. A chain was hooked to a loop at the end of the wire to make sure it wouldn't slip. The winch also had to be made fast, and if possible it was secured with another wire rope to the base of a tree away from the river. Failing that, stakes had to be driven in at an angle to prevent the winch being torn from its moorings by the weight of the tree that was to come down.

Often the only way to saw the tree was by standing up in a boat on the river, not a very comfortable position to saw from at any time, but in the conditions described, fraught with danger as well. Before the sawing started, the strain would be taken up on the winch by two men working the long handle. As the saw bit into the tree an occasional tightening of the wire rope would open up the saw cut, and help the hard-pressed men. A 'face' had to be cut, as in normal tree felling, but this was done after the saw work had progressed a way, and once the face was completed, a further tightening of the wire usually opened the saw-cut a bit more. The most critical and dangerous time was fast approaching, for as the men worked away at the saw, and the winchmen tightened the wire, ominous creaks could be heard coming from the tree. Now was the time for great alertness, but these men knew all the signs, for to a certain extent they depended on their knowledge for survival.

Once the tree had reached a certain point, and it was evident that little more was required to bring it crashing onto the river bank, the men in the boat stopped sawing

70

and retreated to a safe distance. Then the men on the winch would work frantically at the long handle, gradually tightening the wire until the vast bulk of timber toppled over and with a loud crash, shattered its branches as it hit the ground.

One has to see such an operation to appreciate the judgement and skill required to bring it to a successful conclusion. One chap, Joe Williamson, who was foreman of a river board gang, once told me that it was the job he liked least of all amongst the many he had to be responsible for. The danger was great, not only from the tree, but from the wire rope too. Joe told me that once when he was in charge of such an operation, the wire rope snapped under the strain, and if he hadn't been standing behind a tree, the whiplash action of the severed wire would have inflicted grave injuries on him, and might even have cut him in half. The gang were not deterred though, a new wire was found and the job brought to a satisfactory conclusion.

The washing away of the river banks was a job that claimed the attention of these men of the river. A spate of flood water would play havoc with a soft bank, especially on a bend, and these spots had to be repaired. Most river banks have willow bushes growing on them, and these were used to repair damaged banks. The older growth would be cut into lengths, maybe six or seven feet long, and four to six inches in diameter. A number of these would be driven into the river bed across the damaged area, and then the smaller branches and boughs would be interlaced between them, as if making a wattle hurdle. Once this was completed, soil would be built up behind it, by hand of course, and thus the bank was made good. One great advantage of using the available willow was the fact that most of the driven stakes would break into growth in the spring, being in such ideal conditions, and the root growth would anchor the repair work.

Another task that fell to these river workers, was digging out fox earths or badger setts which were sited on a high river bank. A fox might decide to make its home in a bank that had been built up to prevent the flooding of meadow land, but when the river level rose, the holes excavated by

71

reynard or brock acted like pipes through the bank, and in the rush of water, much of the raised bank would be washed away. It was therefore necessary to make sure that reynard and brock took residence elsewhere! The men would have to dig out all the holes and then refill them, firming the soil as they went. Just filling in the holes from the outside would not deter the earth dwellers; a few moments scratching in the dead of night and the work would have been in vain. Today most work along the river banks is done by mechanical means, with a J.C.B. or a small crane taking the place of brawny men, and much seems to have been lost by this progress. Those old timers knew the river in all its moods, for they spent most of their working lives along its banks.

Arthur Thornton was a man who knew every eddy of the water almost, knew all the deep and dangerous spots and knew the pleasure too, of working alongside nature, one could almost say, with nature for fifty years or more. His latter years were spent driving a small machine, which he did not like over much, but before he retired he received the Queen's Jubilee Medal, an award of which he is immensely proud, and rightly so.

The countryside and water have to go together, although sometimes there is too much water, and sometimes not enough. It is rare for our climate to suit all farmers. Some say, 'We could do with rain', and some say, 'Could do with another fortnight of this dry weather'. Wouldn't it be a queer land if everyone had the weather they wanted. Whatever their various requirements, most farmers had to look after the drainage systems on their land. The work was done mostly by the farm-workers and skilled men they were too.

Nearly all hedgerows had a ditch on one side or the other, and it was essential that these ditches should be kept clear, to give a free flow of mainly surface water. Now much of the heavier land in Cheshire was 'butted up'. This means that in a bygone age the field had been ploughed in such a way as to leave ridges and hollows; 'butts' and 'rains'. In the lowest part, the rain was normally a field drain which led to a main drain, which would empty into the ditch. Many of these drains had been dug and piped many years, even a century or more earlier, and naturally it was, at times, necessary to re-dig and pipe some of them, and even to cut a complete new drainage system for a particularly wet piece of land.

Tom Dunning, a farm worker, spent most of his winters at this task on the large farm on which he worked. It was a dirty heavy job needing much skill and brawn. Tom had none of the modern paraphernalia for finding levels and laying out the system, his eyes were enough, for he could judge a 'fall' of even an inch. He would just stick up a few pieces of wood to mark the line of the drain to be laid and start to dig. A number of tools were needed, but the first task was to remove a turf of what ever width was needed for the depth of the trench to be dug. This was done with a 'grafting spade', and the turf placed grass side up some distance from the trench. Next another depth of the spade was dug out and the soil placed alongside the turves. Probably the whole length to be laid would be started like this, and then another tool or rather type of spade came into use, a 'draining tool'. This was a spade wider at the top than the cutting edge, and as another 'spit' or depth of the spade was taken out and placed on the opposite side to the

73

turves, the trench gradually became narrower. If pipes were to be put in fairly deep, perhaps two spits of the draining tool were needed.

The last soil to be removed was the most important, for it determined the depth of the drain and the fall as well. Yet another tool was used, a 'swan neck', which was a kind of spade, or perhaps scraper is a better word, in the shape of a swan's neck. The blade curved so that when used properly it left a curved bottom to the trench for the drain pipe.

Different sizes of 'swan neck' were available for different sized drains, the smallest being three inches, the largest six inches, the size normally used for a main drain. A very good eye was needed to judge just the right amount of fall in a trench up to a hundred yards long, and even the experts would resort to half a bucket of water to test it if the ground to most eyes looked level. Some times the trench would almost fill with water, should the land be particularly wet, which made the pipe laying so much more difficult.

The pipes were put into place with a 'dropper' which was a pole with a rod at the end, bent to an angle to lift a pipe, and it was surprising with what speed the pipes could be laid at the bottom of the trench. They had to be a good fit, for too big a gap between the joins would enable soil to be taken in with the water, and this would naturally hasten the time that the drainage system would require attention. The clay pipes were porous and most of the water soaked through with only a minimum going through the joins, at least if the drain had been well laid.

As most of this drainage work took place during the winter months, there were usually a lot of hedge brushings around, a summer growth, which resulted from the regular maintainance of the hedges. This was not wasted being ideal material with which to cover the pipes. The purpose of this was to prevent much soil being in direct contact with the clay pipes. Next the subsoil was returned to the hole, followed by the top soil, all being firmed down as the work progressed, usually by the drainer who stood in the trench as he proceeded to fill it. It was a pretty dirty heavy job. The turf would be replaced last, and if the job had been well done from start to finish, it would be difficult to find the line of the drain in a few weeks. Old Tom knew where it was though, and he was a most valuable man to have on a farm, since he knew where every drain was, and which ones were most likely to need attention. Tom was so good at his job that sometimes it appeared as if he could make water run up hill! One wonders if the drainage work done with modern machinery and materials will stand the test of time as well as the hard work of men like Tom Dunning. Is yet another country skill lost?

Hedges have always formed an integral part of the rural scene, except of course where stone walls divide parcels of land. Regular attention is needed to keep a hedge in good order, preferably every year. Today in many places a mechanical cutter is used to keep the hedges in good shape, but this does not conjure up the same pleasant rural scene as a gang of men cutting hedges by hand using razor sharp hooks.

Not all the farm hedges were cut every year, some would be left for a year or two, very often those with weaker growth, and these would eventually be laid, a process which will be described later. Labour too was not always sufficient to cut all the hedges, but on an estate it is safe to say that every hedge, with the exception of those due to be laid, were cut without fail. The woodmen formed the workforce that had the task of cutting the many miles of mainly thorn hedge. Frequently the men would be divided into two or three gangs with the senior in charge, and each gang would be alloted its area to cut. The first job was to do the 'copping', the trimming of the base of the hedge and ditch if there should be one. Just a plain 'cop' or bank would be cut with a scythe, but a ditch often needed a smaller tool, a 'copping hook'. The scythe work would be done by an experienced man, but most of the copping would fall to the youngsters, those who had not graduated to a scythe or brushing hook. The men who actually cut the hedge were good at using a hook, or rather a 'brushing' hook. This particular tool came in various forms, with a short blade, long blade, short handle, long handle, curved blade, or bent blade and each man had his favourite form. The medium bladed one on a medium handle was the most popular, being less tiring for a long day's work, but should the hedge have a profusion of brambles entwined amongst it, a curved hook was often the most satisfactory one to use.

A gang of three would do the trimming, starting maybe a hundred yards apart and on opposite sides of the hedge, and the speed with which they would progress along that length was amazing. Once the first length was cut the 'ganger', usually the most experienced man, would take over.

Watty Huxley was such a man, and his skill with almost any woodman's tool was unrivalled. He would weigh up the length, judge the best level at which to cut the top and away he would go. The action he adopted was all his own: swinging the hook in an arc around his head, he would trim that hedge as neat and level as any modern machine and this he would do almost at walking pace! It was rare indeed for him to have to go back to remove any hump.

Left-handed men were not too popular when the gang was hedge cutting, for if by any chance a right-handed man should get that length the following year, it was real hard work. All the cuts would be going the wrong way for the right-handed chap, which meant the hook would not slice easily through the young growth, and some tougher twigs had to be cut as well.

Should a younger man be cutting for the first time, you would hear the older chaps keep saying 'Cut up lad, cut up', for it was incorrect to 'cut down' as that had a tendency to shatter and split the hedge growth, and of course was rather unsightly and not done on an estate where only top class workmanship was acceptable.

One or two of the lads would follow the gang up, and sometimes a real old timer, a man past heavy work, would be amongst them, to rake all the trimmings and debris into heaps which in due course would be carried away by the waggoners. So once more with a summer's growth removed the hedge would look neat and tidy.

There were of course hazards to this job, for it was done in the early autumn when there were still plenty of wasps about and with the shorter days they would be getting a bit

76

drowsy. Many a lad has been stung by the yellow and black peril whilst copping, and often when a particularly strong nest had been disturbed, a length would be left until the nest had been taken out. Each ganger had a small tin of cyanide which was carried for this purpose, and a small piece would be placed in the entrance to the nest when work ceased for the day. The next morning all would be quiet, and that particular length could be finished. Cyanide is of course a poison which gives off a deadly vapour, and it was quite legal to use it to take wasps' nests in those days, but now the most common thing used is 'Cymag', a powder used for gassing rabbits which is equally effective in a wasps' nest.

Often the wasps' nest would be dug out during the lunch break, for the grubs, maggot-like larvae, were most useful as fishing bait, and what lad didn't like a spot of pit or river fishing of an autumn evening.

It was always an aim to keep a hedge of briars, for an excessive growth of these, would certainly produce a nice crop of luscious blackberries. Although if a patch got out of hand, and in fact took over, it would smother the thorn hedge. Despite the prickly nature of the blackberry briar, once the hedge was smothered cattle could quite easily push through and thus create a gap.

The wild, or dog rose was not as bad in this respect, and the single, delicately coloured flowers in the spring and early summer made a wonderful splash of colour. The blooms could be eye-catching with their pastel shades ranging from white to quite deep red, and then in the autumn the 'hips', the bright red seed pods of the rose, gave another hedgerow display. Since the plant provided two colourful displays in twelve months many patches of it were often left in a hedge. However once the patch became too large no mercy was shown, and the whole lot was cut off at ground level, only to make rapid growth the next year, and soon produce another display of blossom. The woodmen and farm workers often made use of this rapid growth for a good strong root stock was an ideal one on which to bud a favourite variety of rose from a cottage garden. Many men were quite expert at this, and with their knowledge of the whereabouts of good stocks, and their

skill at budding, the spring show of rose blooms was maintained in many a cottage garden.

Some hedges, often the weaker ones, were left for a number of years without being cut, so that they could be laid. Now laying a hedge is a rather complicated and skilful operation, but at least it is one of the rural crafts that is maintained today, through competitions that are held all over the country. Usually these competitions take place in conjunction with a ploughing match, and are well worth a visit from anyone interested in rural life.

The laying of a hedge has two main objects: to create a cattle proof fence and to rejuvenate the ageing thorn. Some hedges have existed in the same place for maybe several centuries, and have been laid a number of times over that period. It has been said that it is possible to tell the age of a hedge by the number of varieties of bushes or trees forming that hedge, and it has been calculated that for each hundred years another variety will appear. It is possible to find five or six different things in a hedge, such as white thorn (hawthorn), holly, privet, beech, ash, elder, elm and many more, but it would seem to me that the situation of the hedge probably has a greater bearing on the variety of growth in it than the passing of the years!

Some parts of the country have many hedges consisting mainly of hazel, and these are, quite naturally, easier to lay than a thorn hedge as there are no sharp spikes! Also as the hazel makes a lot of growth each year it was normally the custom not to trim it annually but to lay it again as soon as the growth was long enough. Such hedges are mostly used in sheep country or in corn growing areas, for they would prove but a small obstacle to a rampant cow!

The competition work a hedge-layer prefers is a nice tall well-grown hedge of hawthorn, with little else in the length he is to cut, for should there be, say, a large elder bush, it makes his task more difficult as he will have to fill the gap. The judges would knock a lot of marks off should he fail to do so. It is pleasing that this most skilful of crafts is being kept alive by these competitions, but I am really trying to describe the work of the hedge-layers of long ago. These men did not have to work to such a high standard as the men in today's competitions but they took pride in

78

doing the job well. There were many hedges to be laid, and they would go to visit another man's work, and would not hesitate to pass adverse comments!

Much work was done on a piece work basis, at so much a root, and the price was a matter of agreement, depending to a large degree on the state of the hedge and the type of laying required, for there were several different ways of tackling it. The farmer or estate provided the stakes which were needed every yard or so, but again it was a matter of agreement whether the hedge layer burnt up the debris or not, for it could well be that a field was being drained nearby and the trimmings from the hedge could be used in the process.

The first of the hedge-layer's tasks was to clear all the unwanted growth, and remove any briars or elders that were growing in the hedge. This was often done by an apprentice hedge-layer, but if a tall bushy hedge needed to be thinned before laying could begin, then the craftsmen would always do this, for an inexperienced lad could easily cut away thorn that would be most useful later on. A 'slashing hook' was the usual tool to do this preparatory work, unless some growth of a larger nature needed to be dealt with, when a hard axe would come into play.

Once a reasonable length had been prepared, the hedge-layer would begin by cutting almost through a strong growth, usually at the uphill end should there be one. If at all possible a hedge-layer would always start at the highest point and work downhill. The cut thorn would be twisted over at an angle away from the cut, making sure that a reasonable amount of wood, complete with bark was left undamaged. This was the normal practice, but some-times, a hedge needed to be 'laid off' and brush left on, and for that the 'layer' (cut thorn) would be pushed over at a sharper angle leaving the cut stump completely clear. Another method was to lay the thorns on the same line, and allow the young growth to push through them. This was known as 'on the layers'. Of course, as work progres-sed, it was necessary to drive stakes in to keep the layers in position, and the distance between these could vary with the type of hedge and the material available for laying, but around a yard apart was the usual distance for an average hedge. After a few yards had been laid the craftsman would assess progress and put a few more final touches to the 'pleaches', these being the actual cuts made by the bill-hook, which were always trimmed so that no rough edges were left to rot and angled so that water would run off. Today many cuts are made by the inevitable chain saw, where the old timer would use a hand axe, and these saw cuts leave rough edges as well as a pile of sawdust! Not quite so pleasant to the eye.

When the length was completed, and this took some time at a rate of maybe ten yards a day if the going was good, the final touches were put to the job. Some of the craftsmen would twist withens, hazel or suchlike wands between the stakes at the top of the hedge, to give an almost wattle effect to it, but others would ensure that a good strong layer came to the top as work progressed, and this actually gave a much more natural look. If the hedge was 'laid off' with 'brush', the brush side would be trimmed leaving the effect of a newly cut hedge.

The last task was to rake up and burn all the small twigs and chips, and maybe top up with soil should there be a ditch. The end result would last at least ten years and probably more. I know one hedge that was laid the year 'Tipperary Tim' won the Grand National in the 1920s and it is still a good fence, having been well cared for over all those years.

There were a number of men that I know who were and are top notch hedge-layers: Watty Huxley, Jack Lewis of long ago, and Jack Dunning and Arthur Mort of modern times. All these men have done extremely well in hedge-laying competitions. Watty Huxley in the old days was a champion and eventually he became a judge at such events. Both Arthur Mort and Jack Dunning do well in the local competitions every year. With the exception of the chain saw the tools used today are the same as in the past: bill hook, slashing hook, small and large axes and a rake and pikel to clean up. The men who follow this calling have to be tough for despite the use of thick leather hedging gloves they receive many scratches and worse from the sharp thorns, unless they are lucky and are laying a hazel hedge! Watty Huxley once showed me the back of his hands, which were almost black all over from the many spiky thorns which had caught him. A rum lad Watty, he said, 'There be room for another odd 'un yet.' He also once said, 'We be on this earth to create and pro-create'. Well, he created a good hedge but he had no offspring! A slip-up in his philosophy somewhere.

6 *Of thatchers, blacksmiths, and wheelwrights*

All rural areas had their quota of tradesmen as well as those who followed the more rural crafts: joiners, brick-layers, plumbers, painters, and we mustn't forget the blacksmiths. Many of these men were employed by small building firms, but the larger estates usually had their maintenance department and employed tradesmen of most callings.

This system ensured that the property on an estate was kept in the best possible state of repair, and of course enabled the tenants, mostly themselves estate workers, to have the benefit of any improvements as they came along. There was of course a method by which the work was done, and by dividing the estate into, say five areas, and carrying out repairs and improvements in each area on a five year cycle, there could not be any delapidation.

Sometimes there would be a suitable number of villages on an estate, to enable work to be carried out in a cycle as described. Of course it was necessary from time to time for some of the workforce to work in another area. Perhaps the plumber had burst pipes to attend to or the bricklayer a gale-damaged roof to repair.

These men were practically all country born and bred, and had an interest in all country matters. Often they would be beating when there was a shooting day, helping the farmers out at harvest time, or maybe they would spend a relaxing hour or two by brook, river or pond, 'drowning a worm'. One in particular, a joiner named Alec Taylor, made a hobby of bird watching, and has a most interesting record of birds seen in the area over many years. Of course he has his theories as to why there has been such a dramatic change not only in the varieties of birds, but in their numbers as well, as his records show. Unfortunately theories won't change the situation, but let's hope time does.

Billy Maddocks was a joiner of an earlier generation than Alec. Now one task the joiners had around October every year, was to visit every hunting hatch on the estate. A hunting hatch is a small gate, usually into a wood or in a boundary fence between two farms. These hatches were always locked (with a fitted lock not a bolt), every spring as soon as hunting ceased, and of course they had to be unlocked and put in working order each year before hunting started.

Billy Maddocks and his labourer John Clubbe were assigned this job and eventually came upon a hatch that was in a rather poor condition. However, Billy decided that if the hanging post was renewed and a little work done on the gate, it would be quite serviceable. A new gate post was delivered and John was busy removing the broken one and preparing the hole, whilst Billy was busy planing the new post. Posts for field gates were used unplaned, but a hunting hatch, being used by the hunt was different and was treated as a cottage gate would be. There were shavings everywhere as Billy worked to get the post ready, but then he stopped, in order to measure up his work before putting the post in the hole. John was still busy removing clay from the hole bottom, when he heard Billy roar, 'What's thee done with me two foot?' John had had no measuring to do so had not used the rule, and told Billy so, but no, Billy swore repeatedly that John had had it. John tired of this and got out of the hole, intending to search for the missing item. He immediately saw it. Billy was using it to scratch around in the shavings! Though he was not a bit pleased or amused when told where the supposedly missing item was.

The hunting hatches were always given a lot of attention. The hinges would be greased and the catch made to work freely. It was absolutely essential that once the gate was opened it would not only swing back into a closed position, but the latch would fasten it shut. Such an arrangement made it much easier for the gentlemen following the hounds and of course ensured that a gate would not be left open and enable livestock to ramble.

Another amusing incident involving Billy the joiner was of a rather similar nature. It was the custom for estate employees to have half a day off to go to the races, in this case Chester Races. Well to go was a race itself, involving a bike ride of several miles home, lunch, getting one's best suit on, and then another bike ride into Chester of maybe three or more miles. This particular year Billy was due to go to see the race for the Chester Cup, and he arrived home rather breathless and in a mad rush. He washed and shaved, had a hurried snack and went upstairs to get changed. His wife had laid out his best clothes, his shirt, socks and so on to save him time, but after a few minutes there was a roar from upstairs, 'What yd done with me braces woman?' His wife who was a calm homely person, said, 'Everything has been put out for you Billy.' There was a rattling of drawers, and a fair amount of cursing and stamping could be heard above. Eventually the irate joiner appeared, 'You've hidden the damn things, I knows thee 'as, ye never did want me to go to the races.' 'No I haven't Billy, anyway I want you to put a bob on for me, so hurry up.' Upstairs went Billy and after another vain search he came down again. 'I can't find the b – – – – – things. I'm not going now, its too late,' and he sat down in a chair in a not too happy mood. Sometime later his wife said, 'What's

84

keeping your trousers up Billy?' Billy jumped up only to find that he had his braces on and his shirt over the top! He didn't get to the races but maybe he had the last laugh. The horse he would have put his money on lost, but the one his wife had fancied came home at ten to one, that's the odds not the time! Plumbers always have had a reputation for being forgetful, so perhaps Billy should have been one, but anyway he was a good joiner.

Now plumbers always had plenty of work on an estate. Some estates in the old days had their own water supply network and were entirely responsible for its mainten-ance, from the point at which it left the Water Board main. None of the cottages paid for their water, since it was metered at the point where it entered the estate. This arrangement meant that any waste, such as a dripping tap, was frowned upon, and the estate office had to be told about it at once. The plumbers had plenty of work travelling the estate on cycles, if only to repair or renew worn out washers. They also had to work with the other tradesmen to ensure that everything appertaining to the plumbers' trade was in good order, such as the spouting and down pipes on a cottage, and even the fastening on a cottage wicket which was often 'leaded' into a stone post.

In later years when flush toilets and baths were installed in the cottages, more work was created for this trade, and of course, as these systems were new, they often created a problem or two, which would entail much referring to plans, something an estate plumber was not used to! On one such occasion, a plumber was busy joining two lead pipes using a blow lamp, when his mate who had been studying the relevant plans told him that he was doing it wrong. He put down the blow lamp, and put on his specs for a further study of the plans. The next moment there was pandemonium, as old Bob, the plumber, had put his blow lamp on the window ledge, and the lace curtains were going up in flames! Perhaps plumbers are forgetful after all.

These men can be really indispensable however. On one occasion not many years ago, when the Water Board had become responsible for the mains on the estate, there was a terrific loss of water in one area according to the reading on a meter. The Water Board employees arrived and were busy trying to trace the leak, using modern equipment to do so. After two days of fruitless searching, someone suggested calling in the estate plumber, Bill Ince. Bill duly arrived, and when told what the problem was, without more ado went for his old fashioned 'listening stick'. This stick has one end hollowed like an egg cup, and by prodding the ground with the other, a man with a sensitive ear against the cupped end can hear the 'hiss' of escaping water. Bill set off and in a very short time told the water men to dig in a certain spot. They did so, and soon came upon pretty wet soil, and then the offending pipe. Most of the water was running away in an adjacent field drain, so there was no surface evidence. But Bill Ince knew the course of that particular main pipe and his knowledge solved a problem that the Water Board employees had found very time consuming!

The bricklayers formed an essential part of the clerk of the works department, as there were always plenty of repairs to do, from mending a gale-damaged roof to rebuilding a wall which showed signs of deterioration. They always attended to properties at the same time as the joiners and plumbers, making sure the roof was in good order, and sometimes pointing the brickwork. The chimneys always seemed to need attention, either a new chimney pot was necessary or even at times, the whole chimney stack would need to be repointed or maybe rebuilt.

There was then none of the so-called 'zip up' scaffolding in use today. Scaffolding poles had to be erected if major repairs to a roof were necessary, and of course all material, the mortar, bricks and chimney pots, had to be carried up a ladder. There were no hoists available then, so it was hard work for the bricklayer's labourer as well as for the 'brickie'.

The bricklayers were also responsible for replacing any kitchen grates that had worn out, which did not happen often it must be admitted, for most of them were cast iron ranges, and could cope with the huge fires that were the order of the day. Some are even around today, though I must add, not in use. It could well have been because such large fires were always kept going in the cottages, for logs were readily available, that the chimneys and pots needed attention so often.

As the years passed the bricklayers had the job of replacing the old kitchen ranges with modern grates, which did not need so much fuel, and provided hot water. A brickie and his mate were once engaged on this task in a remote cottage. It so happened that it was market day and the lady of the house always attended. She was of course delighted to be having a modern grate, at no cost, for it was an estate cottage, and as she knew the bricklayer and his mate she asked them if, while they were about it, they would sweep the chimney. Well the old grate was removed, with as little mess as possible, for like most country cottages the room was spick and span, and the time came to sweep the chimney. Tom said 'Fetch those rods John', meaning the draining rods which bricklayers usually carried. John went outside and shortly came back and said, 'We anna git any boss'. Tom was none too pleased having told the old lady that they would 'make a hole through the soot' so he said, 'You 'ad better go to the farm and borrow a set.' John set off to the farm which was about three quarters of a mile away, trudging across muddy fields. In due course he came back, rod-less! 'Their set be at the son's farm,' (a couple of miles away) he told Tom. Now this did not improve Tom's temper a lot and turning on his, by now rather uneasy, labourer, he said, 'You can go and catch that big cockerel off the yard and when you've got him, let me know.' It was no great problem for the labourer, being a country man, to catch the bird. On returning to the cottage he was told to mount the ladder which Tom had placed up to the chimney, and when he received the order, to drop the bird down the soot encrusted orifice. 'I'll be in the kitchen and catch 'ee,' said Tom. In due course down the chimney went the struggling cockerel, sending a dense cloud of soot in front of him and into the face of the waiting Tom. The frightened bird landed with a crash at Tom's feet, and when he made a grab at it through the billowing soot and missed, it took off on a flight round the kitchen. The dust cloths placed with such care over the ornaments and pictures went flying,

87

and when the scared bird eventually escaped through the open kitchen door, there was soot everywhere, as well as all over Tom! What a to-do. Tom blamed John for letting the bird go too soon, but John swore he had waited for Tom to shout. However the mess had to be cleared up, and what a job it was. There was no fire to provide hot water and none of the detergents available today, so they had to use soda and cold water. This of course took some considerable time. The many small china ornaments had to be treated with great care, and everything had to be dried well, leaving no trace of the all-invading black stuff. It was everywhere, on the pictures, behind the pictures, in the vases and even creeping into the drawers of the massive 'dresser'. Eventually the worst had been cleaned up. There was some on the tiled floor, but Tom said, 'T'old lady will expect some about, ye canna sweep a chimney 'bout that'. The new grate was brought in, and in a burst of speed to make up for the spring cleaning session, was soon installed. The two men stood back to admire their achievement, and as they did so, heard the cockerel crow on the yard. Of course they both looked through the window, having forgotten about the unfortunate bird. There he was, perched on a wheel-barrow, shouting his head off. But what a sight! No longer the proud white bird with a large red comb, but a black and white bird, which shed a cloud of soot each time it flapped its wings before crowing. 'Hey John', said Tom, 'Go and ketch him again, we'll have to have him in a bucket of watter.' John set off but of course as soon as the bird saw him approaching, he did a disappearing act into the currant and gooseberry bushes. Both men searched high and low, and eventually found the frightened bird tucked in under a large number of bean sticks which leant against the shed. He was pulled out and taken to the waiting bucket of water. It does not take much imagination to visualize the scene; one man holding the struggling bird, the other trying to wash the adhering soot from the once white feathers. They did not make a very good job of it, but John said, 'Us reckons we'd better put 'un in t'hen house for an hour or so, and let 'un dry off.' This was done, and more satisfied with the situation now, they relaxed over a smoke. There were a few minor things to finish, a bit of pointing round the grate, and a piece of lighted paper to put up the chimney to make sure it drew well. 'It'll draw the cat off the hearth' said John, then it was time to knock off.

The old lady had not got back from market, but this did not matter, for it was quite common and safe to leave a house unlocked in those days. In fact they left the back door open to, 'Clean the smell of soot a bit', said Tom. Away the men went, completely forgetting about the chimney sweeping cock still fastened up in the hen house. The old lady came home in due course, and was delighted with the new grate and the way the men had left the room, for they had replaced the dust covers as if nothing had happened.

A week or so later the bricklayer and his mate were repairing a wall in the area, when who should come along but the old lady from the cottage. She thanked them for making such a good job of the grate and for the way they had left the room, but then said, 'I be a bit puzzled why my cockerel was fastened in the hen house, he was on the yard when I went to market.' Tom thinking quickly said, 'It were us missus, we fastened him in. A strange dog came on the yard and frightened the birds, so we thought it best.' 'Aye, thank ye kindly', said the old lady, 'That accounts for him looking so bedraggled.'

I don't suppose she ever knew the real reason why the bird was fastened up, but perhaps wondered where the soot came from when she next spring cleaned, for the brickie and his mate had not moved any of the furniture!

It was the custom for the bricklayers and labourers to sweep chimneys when working at a cottage, but the favourite way to ensure that the fire would draw well was to use a bough from a holly bush or even a gorse bough. A rope would be lowered down from the chimney pot, the bough tied on, and then pulled through. Great care had to be taken to ensure that the bough was not too big and got stuck half way, but there was no doubt that this method left very little soot behind. When a bough got fast in the chimney it was not unknown for a wisp of burning straw to be dropped down, enough to set fire to the holly or gorse, thus enabling it to be pulled down. This method of clearing a stuck, improvised brush, is not to be recommended with a thatch roof.

Not many estates retained a full-time thatcher, at any rate, not in the part of the country that this book refers to. Any thatched cottage that needed to be re-roofed was handed over to the care of the expert who often travelled a large area of the country. Some cottages were thatched with wheat straw, but most with what was probably the more durable material, Norfolk reed. There is of course a great difference between thatching a stack of corn or hay, and a cottage or other building. The stack is only a temporary job, three or four months is all it has to last, but a habitation needs a more permanent roof.

It is nice to know that there are quite a number still practising the ancient art of thatching. The thatcher likes to select his own material, and in many cases where reed is to be used, will have cut it himself. If straw is to be used, it must be wheat straw and as long and tough as it is possible to get. I should say here that most modern varieties of wheat do not produce a suitable straw for thatching, the main concern being grain, for straw is required less and less, and is often burnt on the fields. The straw from a field of wheat cut by the modern combine harvester is damaged too much for thatching purposes, so the thatcher has to select his crop of wheat from which he can use the straw and arrange for some to be cut in a different way. By cutting the crop with a binder and threshing the grain out using a special machine called a 'comber', the straw is undamaged. Not many farmers are keen to do this, unless of course they have thatched buildings!

The same tools are used today as have been used for centuries, and they are simple but efficient in the right hands. They range from a number of 'hooks' varying in size and shape, to a type of rake, and implements called leggets, which are used to pat and comb the reed or straw into place. Most thatchers use hazel wands to fasten the thatch, but some prefer to use a tarred twine. Two men are needed when twine is used, for one has to pass the twine through from outside the roof, using a thatching needle.

Most thatchers these days are self employed but they always have been 'individuals'. Most had their own style, and often specialized in one particular material, usually that produced in their part of the country. At the same time, a good man could produce an excellent job from reed, straw or even heather or sometimes bracken. The life of these various materials varies. Reed, if maintained properly, can last for the best part of a century, straw maybe forty years or so. I understand that the largest thatched building in Britain is a tithe barn in Wiltshire which requires over two hundred tons of Norfolk reed. Five experts take several months to complete the task of rethatching it.

A well-thatched house, cottage or building, is a pleasure to look at, and there are still many around, mostly in the southern half of the country. Let's hope the skill of the thatcher will never be lost, for despite the use of slate, tile and other roofing materials, there must always be a place for such a picturesque building as a well-maintained thatched cottage.

The countryside has always had its village blacksmith, even if the villages didn't all have a spreading chestnut tree. The blacksmiths formed an integral part of country life but unfortunately in modern times there are fewer and fewer of them. Some have survived by adapting to modern needs and perhaps should be called agricultural engineers, for most of their work is with modern farm machinery. Welding equipment is probably more important to them than the old time forge.

A blacksmith's shop was often the focal point of a village, for at some time or other all the inhabitants would be in need of his services. The farmers and their men were regular customers and what better time could you have to exchange gossip than whilst a farm horse was being shod, for there was no doubt that the village 'smith knew as much about the goings-on in the area as anybody, unless it was the landlord of the local hostelry! If old so-and-so brought his plough in for repair, then he was about to till the land, and if somebody else came in for a new 'spout' for his corn drill, this meant he was going to be sowing shortly. For some unknown reason an implement seldom came in for repair until it was actually needed, often lying in a broken condition all winter!

A blacksmith occupying a smithy on an estate was in a pretty secure position, for he was almost certain to get the bulk of the estate work, from repairing wrought iron gates to making staples and clasps for field gates, and sometimes even making nails for a special job. There would be a large number of farm horses which had to be shod at regular intervals. Knowing all the horses which he shod in the area, the blacksmith would have large numbers of shoes ready made, probably a set for each horse, and when one arrived at the smithy, a set was ready, only needing to be heated and adjusted to make a perfect fit. This system saved the customer time and also gave the blacksmith a job during any slack period.

A part of a good smith's craft was the ability to make wrought iron gates and railings, and of course repair them. Most large estates had massive gates at the drive entrances, and since many of these were made a century ago, parts at times needed to be replaced. The damaged piece would be removed, taken to the smithy and a replica made. Once back in position it could not be told from the original. There are of course firms that specialize in making so-called wrought iron gates, but by and large, they are not 'wrought iron' as the old smith would term it, so much as bent or twisted strips of mild steel, often done with the use of a template. It is not easy to describe the difference, but the strip metal is usually just cut across, whereas the blacksmith's wrought iron was narrowed and thickened at the end, and when say, a gate was made, it would be a much more attractive sight than its modern counterpart.

Nowadays, a real wrought iron gate would cost a fortune in labour charges alone, whereas, the thin strips and modern construction methods of today's version make it comparatively cheap, even though its life must be shorter.

A 'knacky' man was the village blacksmith. Using scrap metal he would make many useful items such as a 'staple drawer', a most useful tool when staples that had been driven home had to be taken out. This was often made from a worn-out rasp, of the type used to pare a horse's foot before shoeing. By heating the rasp in the forge and by the dexterous use of a hammer, the smith formed a hook at one end. This could be driven under the staple, and the length of the rasp gave leverage to withdraw it. No farm could afford to be without this handy piece of recycled metal.

Another thing the smith would make was a wire strainer, which was a bit more complicated than a staple drawer, but nearly always made of scrap metal of which no smithy was ever short. Two hooked pieces of iron were fastened by a chain to a longer piece and by placing the hooks over the wire in a certain way, it was possible, by using the long piece as a lever, to tighten the wire to the required tension. Small plates of metal fastened to a longish rod made 'rakes' for cleaning out the fire grates and of course a poker for the fire was easy!

I mentioned earlier that the setting of a scythe blade was an important task, and of course there were many other tools that came in for the attention of the blacksmith. It would seem to be a job for a joiner to put new handles on broken tools such as spades, forks and hooks of all descriptions, but most men preferred the smith to do the job for them. Of course there was a reason for this. A new handle was always a much better fit if the metal had been heated, and tapped gently to conform to the new wood-work. Also the broken part could more easily be removed after a few moments in the forge. One suspects also that the countryman looked forward to a while in the smithy.

The old time smithy with its forge, and smell of singed hooves and hot metal was always an attractive place to be, especially on a cold day, not only for the men working the land but for the village lads as well. Many a youngster has spent an hour or two by the forge, working the bellows which forced the draught through the coke to produce an almost white-hot heat. This very high temperature was essential to make thick metal malleable under the black-smith's hammer, and even a horseshoe had to be heated many times in the forge before it was finished.

Today where forges like this are used the draught is provided by pressing a button on an electric motor which works a fan, although many jobs are done using 'gas' and a blow torch. There are mobile forges which tour an area to shoe the ponies which are so popular with children, but by and large, the men who use these are farriers not blacksmiths, and they are often in great demand especially in 'hunting country', for a hunter must be well shod at all times.

With the advent of the motor car the work of the wheelwright started to decline, and today he is in even less demand than the blacksmith. At one stage, it was not at all uncommon for the wheelwright to do the blacksmith's work, and vice versa. It was a very skilled job making, let alone repairing, an old steel rimmed wheel. I suppose it was in a way a combination of the blacksmith's and the joiner's work. The woodwork used in making a wheel was of at least two sorts. Elm owing to the way the grain runs in many directions, was always used for the hub, and the spokes would normally be made of oak, this being a very strong timber. The wooden rim was often made of ash and this had to be made in a number of sections.

I do not intend to go into the methods of making a wheel, or the number of tools needed from a lathe for making the hub, to an edge for trimming and various clamps to hold the parts in place. Perhaps fitting the metal rim or tyre is the most exacting part of making a wheel. This rim has to be made very accurately for if it is small it will cause the spokes of the wheel to go out of alignment and the work will be ruined.

The rim is heated until red hot, and then, held in tongs, is placed over the rim of the wheel and hammered into place. As this happens it is doused with cold water, not only to put out the flames from the burning wood but to cool the metal, making it contract and tighten on the wheel. I have heard the wheel creaking as the metal cools, but this is a good sign, for it means that the contracting metal is tightening up the joints and the rim or tyre should remain in position for many years.

The blacksmith could be heard at work over a wide area. As he hammered metal on the anvil the ringing notes wafted through the air almost like the church bells. Nearly all smiths seemed to use the same method when hammering out metal on the anvil; two blows on the metal and then two blows on the anvil, those were the ringing tones that could be heard so far. I asked the local blacksmith, Wilf Broster, why all smiths seemed to do this, and he replied

94

with a sly grin, 'Well we've got to let the hammer cool down haven't we?' Now I don't know if this is the reason, or whether Wilf, never at a loss for words, came out with the first thing in his head!

Most country blacksmiths were fond of rural sports, particularly hunting, for of course they shod most of the hunting horses! It was not unusual to see a smith riding a horse when the hounds were out, not that many of these craftsmen could afford to own a horse suitable for hunting, but often a local gentleman would loan him one for a day's sport.

Shooting was a sport that Wilf Broster was particularly fond of and he was an excellent shot. Most of his activities in this field were limited to pigeon and rabbit shooting, and he often had invitations from the local farmers when these were plentiful. Clay pigeon shooting was something at which he excelled, winning numerous trophies and cups at local shoots over a long period. Yes blacksmiths by and large were sporting men, and for some reason, most of them were not averse to a 'bob on the horses'. Maybe they often had a little inside knowledge, for some, Wilf included, were frequently called upon to 'plate' local race horses (plating is shoeing, where a race horse is concerned) and thus had to chance to turn a bob into a pound!

Those old time blacksmiths were indispensable but it is doubtful if any of them did more than make a decent living. Most of them worked hard and played hard, but almost certainly they would not have changed their lives for anything.

Most villages of any size had their smithy and it was the custom for it to be handed down from father to son. In a small area of Cheshire I have known a number of blacksmiths over the years: Dick Danger, Bill Pierce, Jacky Thomas and the aforementioned Wilf Broster. Perhaps I knew Wilf best of all, so to conclude this chapter I will relate a true story that in a small way was typical of the man. He has unfortunately passed on without a son, and the smithy has closed.

A mutual friend, one Thomas Broster, (a distant relation of Wilf) was prone to heavy colds during the winter months, and indeed some winters these infections were so bad they would turn to bronchitis. Tom blamed this on the privations he had endured during his long and distinguished service throughout the Second World War. One particularly miserable winter with a lot of cold, wet, windy weather, Tom had to take to his bed as usual, shortly after Christmas with a real heavy cold, which in due course turned to bronchitis. He was a popular jovial man, and of course when he was not in circulation he had plenty of visitors to his sick bed. This particular evening I had called to see how he was progressing, and his wife sent me up to his bedroom. There was Tom, propped up in bed with the usual bottle of Lucozade (Tom would have preferred something stronger) and a number of books, for he was a great reader. He looked quite well and said that he'd be up in a day or so. As we discussed various local matters and I tried to keep him up to date with village affairs, we heard voices in the kitchen below. Tom said, 'Hush I know that voice, I'm damn sure it's Tiny's.' Tiny being Wilf Broster's nick-name, which was only to be expected as he was six feet three! Sure enough a minute or so later, Tom's wife, May, shouted from the bottom of the stairs, 'Another visitor Tom.' 'Send 'im up', shouted Tom, a sure sign that he was on the mend, for a sick man is not inclined to shout too loud.

Then could be heard the thump thump of Wilf's size eleven shoes as he started upward. There was a pause about half-way up, for many staircases in this particular village did a complete circle to the upper floor, and no doubt Wilf had paused to think, for shortly after he shouted up to Tom in the bedroom, 'Tell you what Tom, these would be damned awkward stairs to get a coffin down'. Now it didn't strike me as a very funny remark, but Tom roared with laughter, in fact he laughed so much he started coughing, and of course when he laughed so infectiously we all had to join in. Tom incidently was a rotund man of twenty-three stone.

After regaining his composure Tom said, 'Eeh mester, what you brought us?' Wilf said, 'Nowt, what do you want?'. 'I wouldn't mind a nice nip' said Tom. 'Reet' says Wilf, and left the room. About ten minutes later he returned with a whiskey bottle, I nearly said a bottle of whiskey, but it wasn't that, for there was just enough in it for a decent drink apiece!

Thomas Broster was soon on his feet and back at work, so perhaps the joke helped, or was it the whiskey, or was it both?

7 *The business of gamekeeping*

The gamekeeper's job was always looked upon as a glamorous and, perhaps more correctly, a secretive one. By and large there was not and is not much glamour about it, but by its very nature it had to be a bit secretive. In a way a gamekeeper on an estate was also the 'policeman' of the fields, for his role was not completely taken up by looking after the game.

The old time keepers were, inevitably, a different class of men from their modern counterparts, and in many ways they were much closer to nature, for with only their two feet to get about on they saw and heard much more than the modern keeper in the inevitable Land Rover.

Dress was an important thing in the old days, for a landed gentleman who employed gamekeepers was sure to have a distinctive livery. In most cases the gamekeepers were issued with two suits of clothes, one for work, and one for ceremonial occasions, such as shooting days. The working suit would be of real hard-wearing material, capable of standing up to the sharp thorns of briar bushes and other undergrowth. It was usually made of a very heavy cord which was almost impervious to water, for there was no waterproof clothing then. A keeper was thus well protected from both the harshness of the woodlands and the weather as well. A darkish grey or a brown were the colours most favoured, for on many occasions it was essential that the wearer should be able to melt into his surroundings. A black hard hat, a waterproof piece of head-gear if ever there was one, and either boxcloth or leather leggings completed the outfit. With his gun under his arm, or a stout ashplant to help him on his way, and a faithful dog walking to heel, he conjures up a picture of a bygone era.

On a shooting day, when, more than likely there would be titled and famous gentlemen present to enjoy the sport, it was a different suit the keeper wore. In most cases it would be made of velvet, and this is probably where the notion of glamour came in. The green of the jacket and waistcoat only emphasised the shine on the brass buttons, which on closer inspection would be found to be embossed with the crest of the landowner, should he be entitled to one. White breeches and white boxcloth leggings made the green velvet stand out, and with his black bowler hat, liberally banded in gold braid, the keeper made an altogether impressive picture. The quantity of gold braid on the hat indicated the position of each individual gamekeeper; one band for an underkeeper, two bands for a beat keeper, and three for the man in charge, the headkeeper.

This was the pattern followed by most large estates, though of course there were many variations on the same theme, depending on perhaps, the position in society of the owner or maybe his financial state. The suit of clothes described above would cost a large sum of money by the standards of those days, and as ten or even more gamekeepers were often employed, there was a fairly hefty bill from the tailors!

Naturally when a ceremonial suit was showing signs of wear, it was replaced, and the old one worn on more mundane days. For this reason gamekeepers of a bygone age were called 'Old Velveteers'. One old keeper I knew, called Joe Saint, wore a hard hat at all times, and the workaday one had seen so much service in fair weather

99

and in foul that the original black colour had taken on a lovely green hue. When asked why he persisted in wearing such delapidated head-gear, he replied, 'Them as I want to see, canna' see me so easy when me 'ed is hid by lichen.' True enough, a green hat would not show up as much as a black bowler in woodland.

The skills of a gamekeeper are numerous, and there is no doubt that the old timer needed more than his modern counterpart. Nets formed an essential part of his equipment, and it was rare indeed to find a keeper who could not knit his own nets. Purse nets, which were used when ferreting rabbits, were needed in large numbers and replacements had to be made; then there were long nets for netting rabbits at night. A long net took quite some time to make, being usually around fifty yards long, and a yard deep, and so great care was taken of it. Any broken mesh was repaired for it was not at all unusual to get a net entangled in debris at night. A partridge net was not used as much as a purse or long net, and it often happened that if a net of this description was in a keeper's possession he had taken it from poachers!

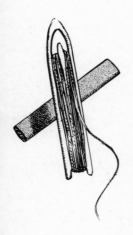

Net knitting is not a difficult task. Once the basic method has been learnt, making a long net is then only a matter of patience. The same simple tools are used that have been used throughout the world for centuries. Where nets are produced commercially, the making of them is usually called 'braiding' but the keepers always said they were going to knit a net. The needle used was called a netting needle or sometimes a braiding needle. This and a mesh pin were all that were needed in the making of a net, plus the twine of course! The mesh pin (sometimes called a measuring stick) determined the size of the mesh, and came in various sizes according to the mesh needed. For rabbit nets the mesh would be around two inches. The twine used could be of hemp, cotton or flax, but I once took a long rabbit net off poachers that had been made of a silky twine, similar to that used for old-style fishing lines, and very light and effective it turned out to be.

The needle would vary in length, but was usually around six inches for the average mesh. A small needle needed to be threaded frequently for a skilled operator could tie as many as thirty meshes in a minute. Once the net had been cast on and secured to an immovable object, the most important thing was to ensure that all the knots were of an even tension which is where skill and judgement were required.

Long nets were almost certainly the most effective way of catching a number of rabbits quickly and with a minimum of effort, in the days when the whole countryside was overrun with conies. On the right night, (these nets had to be used in the dark) it was quite possible to catch a hundred or so in less than an hour, and they were of course all nice clean rabbits, free of lead shot. The wind had to be blowing into the wood to be netted, so that the rabbits out in the fields feeding were less likely to hear any noise made by the keepers, or for that matter poachers! Three was the ideal number of people for this operation. One man ran the net out, letting it fall freely off a peg, only pausing to give a slight tug on it to take up any slack. A second man followed pegging the yard-deep net up, usually with hazel pegs, to a height of about two feet. The third man remained at the starting point, holding the top line of the net. When the whole net was run out and pegged he would feel a tug on the line which was a signal to start drawing the feeding bunnies into the waiting net. Then a man would set off sideways from each end of the net, until the extreme of the field was reached. A very low 'ssh, ssh' or sometimes the rattling of a box of matches was all that was needed to send the conies scuttling for safety, only to be entangled in the net, where the third man dealt with them.

If there were only two men on a netting expedition, a long line called a 'banting' line would sometimes be used to drive the conies to the net. It was pegged firmly at one end of the net, then payed out as progress was made to the far side of the field, and finally dragged across the grass on the way back, thus ensuring that any feeding bunny made a hasty retreat. It was great fun netting rabbits at night, but alas, perhaps the farmers wouldn't say so. Nowadays, in many areas there aren't enough for such an expedition to be mounted. A skilled trio could set a hundred yards of nets, (two fifties) drive in, gather the catch, pick up and be away in no more than twenty minutes, and more than likely have as many rabbits as they could carry!

Netting rabbits at night was greatly favoured by prewar keepers, for they were really doing two jobs at once. If it was the right sort of night, with a fair breeze blowing, a hint of rain in the air, and of course ground that was free of frost, it was almost certain that poachers would be operating. Now on most estates the keepers were responsible for the control of rabbits, and long netting on a suitable night helped in that respect. There was also a chance that poachers would be after rabbits too and so the keepers would get the opportunity to catch them as well as the conies.

Whilst writing about rabbits and gamekeepers snaring comes to mind, and if there was an expert at making and setting snares, it was the keeper. Most preferred to make their own snares, a fairly simple process once the knack had been acquired. The simple method required two pointed pegs about a foot long, and a coil of thin brass wire. One peg was placed over a small stone or piece of wood on the ground, and the other held in the hand, on the knee. The brass wire was then run around these two pegs until the required number of strands had been obtained. Each keeper had his favourite number of strands, either six or eight. After the wire had been fastened off by twisting round the strands, and removed from the wooden pegs, there was a loop at each end, where the wire had been round the peg. One loop was pushed through the other creating a noose, a strong loop of string attached to free loop, and then fastened to a stout peg. With the stout peg driven into the ground near a rabbit run, and the noose placed in a small thin 'pricker? peg' about four inches from the ground, over the rabbit run, the snare was set.

Rabbits were snared throughout the winter months, and often a keeper would set as many as a hundred snares at a time, in one or sometimes a double line, some distance from a wood. If the snares were set in the morning a great deal of the human smell had dispersed by dusk, and just as the shades of night were falling was a good time to look the snares. No light would be needed, and as there would be many rabbits out feeding, quite a lot would fall foul of the snares as the keeper appeared on the scene. Re-setting any snares that had caught made another capture possible during the night. As daylight broke, the keeper would be there again to collect the snared rabbits, and it was not unknown for there to be as many rabbits taken as there were snares set. After a couple of days the snares would be moved to another spot and the process repeated.

Some people say that snaring should be banned because of the cruelty involved. I suppose it is inevitable that there is some cruelty, but an experienced man will set the snares in such a fashion that the victim dies almost instantly by breaking its neck. This is really to the snarer's advantage too, for a rabbit caught by the body could squeal for some time, and would attract any foxes in the area, from even a mile away. If this happened, the rabbit might be left, half eaten, and more than likely the snare would be either broken or pulled up! This is no use to the keeper who then has to make more snares, but he would have learnt that there was a reynard in the area!

It is not really possible to describe how a snare is set to kill quickly, so much really depends on the terrain, and

where on the run a snare is set, and of course the size of the loop in the snare. You will read in some books that four fingers high to the bottom of the snare is correct for a rabbit, and the height of an outstretched thumb for a hare (about two inches higher). In fact this is only a rough guide for the beginner, for only practice will bring about the ability to snare effectively. Even where there are reasonable numbers of rabbits, there are probably not enough of them for anyone to get enough experience to be an expert snarer in one season, as was the case in the days before myxomatosis.

Most pictures or drawings of a gamekeeper show him carrying a gun and with a dog at heel. This is fair enough, but although a gun is an essential part of a keeper's equipment he does not carry it anywhere near as much as the pictures suggest. When on patrol, however, particularly in the spring, or when looking at his tunnel traps, he is most likely to have a gun under his arm, for an opportunity may present itself for dealing with a predator, such as a carrion crow or stoat.

At one time nearly all keepers loaded their own cartridges, for they often needed one or two cartridges with a particular load of shot for a special job. Apart from that it was normal for a gamekeeper to be supplied with powder and shot, and he would re-cycle the cartridge cases again and again, making the necessary wads from any old pieces of cardboard and felt. Many of the prewar cartridge cases were made entirely of brass, and this was for shot gun ammunition not rifle. These cases were loaded many times until there was no card lining to be turned over the shot-retaining wad. Several tools were needed for reloading cartridges. One extracted the used 'cap' and usually this implement could be reversed to put a new cap in the case. Two measuring 'cups' which could be adjusted to various amounts of shot and powder, according to requirements, were used to measure out first the powder and then the shot, and of course punches were required to cut the wads. When cap, powder, felt wad, shot and cardboard wad had been replaced in the case, an implement was needed to turn the rim of the case over on to the cardboard wad. This was normally clamped

104

onto a table, the case pushed in a tube and the end turned over by a number of turns on a handle.

Today of course there is much less home-loading of cartridges. It is doubtful if there is a gamekeeper to be found who does this, nor are there many of the old tools around, unless they are in a museum. Modern equipment is available at a price, but unless a person uses very large numbers of cartridge, it can hardly be a viable proposition. Maybe clay pigeon shooters can make use of modern tools, but even so many competitions stipulate that cartridges bought on the ground must be used, so home-loaded ones would be of little use, even for practice. Some Wild Fowling clubs have I know, purchased a machine for their members, and no doubt it makes for cheaper ammunition for the men who go after the elusive ducks.

Trapping all sorts of wild life was commonplace in the old days, in fact it was an integral part of a gamekeeper's job. Today, for many reasons, there is not the same necessity to trap on a large scale. In fact many of the old methods are illegal, and this is a good thing. The old 'gin' trap, for instance, has been banned for many years. This was the trap that was used in rabbit holes, and accounted for literally millions of conies over the years. It was also used in 'tunnel' traps to catch ground vermin or predators as they are called today.

A tunnel trap is exactly what it says: a trap in a tunnel. Keepers would build such tunnels at the junction of two hedges, at the base of stone walls or in gaps in walls, and would also use any natural hole, such as one into a hollow tree. A trap placed in such a position would be 'working twenty-four hours' in the words of one old keeper, and would take a heavy toll of stoats, weasels, rats as well as the odd rabbit. Much skill was needed in siting such a trap, and a vast knowledge of nature, for what might appear to be a perfect spot would catch very little and another most unlikely place would get catch after catch. An experienced gamekeeper using a comparatively small number of such traps would keep ground vermin under control. The smaller the number of traps, the easier his task, for it was essential that each trap should be looked at every day.

105

The 'gin' trap could cause suffering to any victim, for in most cases a leg or legs would be trapped in the metal spring-held jaws, and only the smaller mammal, say a weasel, would be trapped by the body and die fairly quickly, if not instantly. This trap, when banned, was replaced by an unwieldy trap called the 'Juby', which, although effective in a rabbit burrow, was not at all useful in a tunnel. The other trap, the 'Fenn', which became available at the same time is much easier, not only to handle, but also to set. This trap is used by the modern keeper in tunnels as described, but despite its claim to kill instantly the luckless mammals that fall foul of it, in my experience less than half die a sudden death, and it is in fact not a very great improvement on the old fashioned gin. The Fenn has no ragged edges on the jaws, and consists merely of stout wire, but it has a strong spring that will damage a trapped leg almost as badly as its predecessor, the iron gin trap.

Tracking both wildlife and man was a skill used much more in the past than in the present. It was, and for that matter still is, important that a keeper should know what was afoot on his patch, and one way was to identify tracks left in muddy ground, for nearly everything has to put its feet on the ground at some time, birds included. Flattened grass and herbage will also indicate the passage of some person or animal, and it is surprising how far such evidence can sometimes be followed. Human beings provide clearer evidence of their passage than most animals, for it is true that many folk, particularly those who do not live in the country, walk through a muddy or damp patch instead of going round it. Thus a footmark in a muddy place, maybe in a gateway, will give an observant keeper more information than one might suspect. The size and shape will of course indicate whether it was made by a man, woman or child, and the depth of the mark in the mud will tell the approximate build of the person. The density of the mud also has to be taken into account as the mark will be deeper in sloppy mud than in thick gooey stuff. The direction the person has taken is pretty obvious, and by following up, it is often possible to find out why the visitor has been there at all.

A gamekeeper was once talking to a farm worker in the local hostelry, mainly about things of mutual interest. After a while the conversation began to dry up, most topics having been exhausted, when something dawned on the keeper, 'You've got a new pair of boots then Jimmy,' he said. Looking down at his feet Jimmy replied, 'Nay these are shoes, I've had 'em years.' 'Ah, but the boots you work in' said the keeper, 'What about them?' 'Oh aye, had a new pair a week or so ago,' said Jimmy. 'Thought so' said the keeper, 'Gone in for a good pair haven't you, Zug I reckon?' 'Aye that's reet. Missus had a spare bob or two, so I got some tidy uns. But how did 'ee know?' The keeper smiled and replied with a raucous 'Aarrh' and never did enlighten Jimmy. The keeper had seen fresh footmarks in a gateway two days running and knew that that was Jimmy's route to fetch the cows up for milking, and he also knew the pattern of the hobnails on the soles of the boots, which were pretty distinctive. He was almost certain a pair of Zug boots had been on the feet of the person who had passed that way, and after the conversation in the pub he knew that that person had been Jimmy, and that Jimmy's wife had contributed to the quite expensive, but waterproof and hardwearing footwear! Quite a bit of information from two tracks in the mud!

The same keeper, me!, once spotted where someone had been digging a rabbit out of a small burrow, and naturally took note of the tracks in the soft disturbed earth. A day or two later I saw two men coming across a field, about a mile from the dug out rabbit burrow, and they looked a bit suspicious. I got to a position where they would walk up to me, and as they did so I asked them their business. 'Only been for a walk boss,' said one. Now his pockets had a definite bulge, so I said, 'Let's have a look at what you have in your pockets.' 'Nay,' he said, 'You'll only take it from us, it's a rabbit.' While this conversation was taking place, I noticed that their footmarks corresponded to those I had seen on the rabbit burrow a day or two earlier. 'Were you in the Fox Covert a couple of days ago?' I asked them. 'No, not us' was the reply. I then told them that I knew they were. 'You've got to put your feet on the ground haven't you?' I said. They didn't know what to make of that remark but after a pause one said, 'You're not going to "do" us, are you?' I said, 'No, you won't be summonsed this time, but don't come again.' To the best of my knowledge they never did.

To the average country dweller, tracks in mud are not at all interesting, but to a keeper they are an open book, and to be able to decipher these indentations is an essential skill. An ever-changing pattern is made by wildlife as it moves about its day to day business. The difference in the tracks of the male and female of any one species is surprising, but the keeper can tell. I do not propose to try to describe here the various subtle differences in these tracks, for there are several illustrated books on the subject. Most of the photographs in these books have been taken of very plain or rather clear imprints, for obvious reasons, but actual observation in the field is a rather different matter. The type of ground on which the tracks are seen will make a lot of difference, and can vary from rain or even dew dampened dust, to really sloppy mud. Each surface will alter footmarks, and of course the speed at which an animal or a running bird is travelling, will make a surprising difference too.

Another factor that has to be taken into consideration is the time of the year. The track of a fox is probably one of the easiest to recognise, but there is a distinct difference between the size of a dog fox's pad and that of a vixen. The vixen's is quite a bit smaller, but around September, when the cubs of that season are on the move, a young dog fox's tracks can easily be mistaken for those of an old vixen, so although the layman would probably be able to say, 'A fox has passed this way', it would take an experienced keeper to know if it was a young dog fox.

Birds are less inclined to leave tracks in the mud, but game birds, pheasants and partridges, spend much of their time seeking food on the ground, and are bound to pass through mud or damp soil, thus giving useful information to the vigilant keeper. It is not quite so easy to tell the difference between the tracks made by male and female birds, and even young birds very soon have feet of a similar size to those of their parents.

The tracks of the inhabitants of the countryside are not

the only things that give a gamekeeper information of what is going on. Birds in particular are always giving indications of what is happening in the area which they have made their territory. Most of them have a number of alarm calls, all of which can mean the presence of a predator, and the intensity of the call usually indicates how close the enemy is. Some birds, blackbirds for instance, have different alarm notes for a predator on the ground, and for a predator of the air, such as an owl. A piping note, 'chink, chink, chink' is a sure sign that a four-legged enemy is afoot, be it fox, stoat, weasel, cat, rat or sometimes even a skulking dog. A rather deep 'tschuch, tschuch' is more likely to indicate a winged predator which has settled in a nearby bush or tree. This particular call can be confused by the inexperienced, with the 'chac, chac, chac' which the cock blackbird invariably makes just before going to roost.

Many birds have alarm calls but few are as noisy when protesting about an invasion of their territory as the blackbird. The blue tit has one very high-pitched note, not audible to every human ear, that indicates that a hawk, usually a sparrow hawk, is flitting through the trees. One wonders if other birds can hear this high-pitched sound, or whether only members of the tit tribe know to seek safety in a suitable spot.

I have tried to indicate the knowledge that is most useful to a gamekeeper, although it has to be admitted that a modern day 'velveteer' has not the same need of nature lore.

As well as tracks in the mud and birds' alarm notes in the trees, herbage provides quite a lot of information to the person with an inquiring mind. Thistle heads that have plainly been attacked by birds are an almost certain indication that there are goldfinches on the move, for the seeds of the scotch thistle are a favourite item of that colourful bird's diet. Toadstools that have been partly eaten and show teeth marks probably indicate the presence of a grey squirrel, for it is a great forager and will eat a large variety of things. As is well known, it stores nuts, grain and even quite small seeds. Most of these stores are never visited again by the squirrel, but provide many a good feed for the ever present mice. Perhaps the squirrel has a poor memory, but it is more likely that during most English winters, the need to visit the stores does not arise. Squirrels can be seen busy foraging during the winter months, for any sunny day will bring them out of their dreys.

Rabbits make runs on their way out to feed, and where there are a large number of conies, these are very plain to see. However most mammals make runs of one sort or another which are not so obvious. A trained eye is needed to spot where a stoat, for instance, is running regularly, but the gamekeeper needs this information to enable him to deal with the predator. Rats, should they invade a certain spot, soon give away their presence by their well-trodden runs, and in the old days it was the practice to snare these rodents. Quite a simple snare was used, but the method of setting differed from most other snaring techniques. The rat is a great animal for chewing its way through most materials, and as it was very difficult to snare a rat in such a way that it died quickly, using the ordinary method, a type of spring had to be used. When a rat entered this type of snare, the tension on the snare itself disengaged it from a notched peg driven into the ground, and snare and rat flew into the air, for they were attached to a springy stick, about four feet long. This stick had been driven firmly into the ground, and with the snare attached to the end, bent over and its end engaged in the smaller notched peg. The weight of the rat suspended in mid-air caused a speedy death, with little or no suffering.

It is doubtful if this method of snaring rats is used today, although as far as I know is still legal. It is much easier to use the proprietary poisons which are readily available, and which, if used correctly, are much more effective.

Herbage which has been trodden down eventually creates a run, for example the path made by the partridge going to its nest. An expert eye can detect the movements of many things. Perhaps this is most easily demonstrated early in the morning when there is a heavy dew. Anything walking through this water-laden grass knocks the drop-lets off, and thus the grass appears a different shade of green from the dew laden area which reflects the light. This is easy to spot when the dew is present, but once the

110

dew has evaporated, all the grass appears the same shade, or more or less the same shade of green. However the individual blades of grass have been slightly bent. This is not easy to spot, but the real good 'tracker' can do so, and can even follow these tracks for a considerable way.

The foregoing has indicated some of the skills a good keeper needs, but there are many others. The rearing of game, pheasants, partridges and even ducks, is a much more simple and certain business than of yore; modern equipment and feed see to that. Partridges in particular were not easy to rear in the old days, when little was known about proteins. It was known that most game birds ate a vast number of insects of all sorts during their first ten days of life, and it was also known that wild partridges were particularly fond of ant eggs. If there were ant hills in the area a keeper who was trying hard to rear partridge chicks hatched under broody hens, would go and shovel these ant hills into sack bags. These would be emptied out near the coops holding the fluffy chicks, and in a short while not only the ant eggs but the ants as well would be gobbled up by the eager young partridge. Along the railway embankments was a favourite place to gather these ants and their eggs, for in one particular area the sandy soil was ideal. After getting permission from the railway authorities, forays were made twice a week. As it was two or more miles away a horse and 'float' had to be used, and this was usually stabled at a near-by farm whilst the ant hills were bagged. About twenty bags, each holding around half a hundredweight were filled, this being the limit the float horse could haul. About ninety nine point nine per cent of this was soil with only a few eggs and ants! On one occasion, disaster struck when the usual bags had been filled, and the transport collected from the nearby farm.

The nearest route home entailed going over a hump backed bridge, which was indeed very humped, rather like those of pack-horse days, and spanned the Shropshire Union Canal. The horse and float, with its load of ants' nests, keeper and assistant approached this bridge at a steady pace, which was reduced to a crawl on arrival at the steep incline. Blazes, the horse, made steady progress until she reached the crown of the bridge, and then as she

111

took her first step down hill her legs went from under her, and she was pinned to the ground by the shafts of the float. Charlie Worthington, the keeper, and his assistant jumped out, rather at a loss as to what to do. The assistant suggested unloading the float and getting Blazes back on her feet. Charlie would have none of it 'We'll get her out, you undo the harness.' Well this was much easier said than done as the assistant soon found out, for the weight of the float and its load was pinning everything down, and making all the buckles as tight as drums. After much struggling and not a little cursing, Blazes was freed, none the worse for the mishap. Once again the assistant suggested removing the bags from the float. 'No,' said Charlie, 'You lead the horse to the bottom of the bridge and I'll get the float down.' Away went the assistant until he reached a spot where the lane widened, where he waited to see how Charlie fared with the float. After a considerable struggle the float could be seen to be on the move, with Charlie between the shafts. To start with progress was slow, but as soon as the full weight got moving down the incline, Charlie's step had to lengthen, and gradually it became longer and longer. Then Charlie started to run, his stride lengthening all the while. After about ten yards Charlie was moving as if wearing 'three league' boots, and he had obviously lost control. On and on he went until reaching a point about fifty yards beyond, where the lane joined a main road, and here Charlie shot straight across the road, clinging desperately to the shafts of the float.

The assistant gazed wide-eyed, as Charlie disappeared into a ditch and the float, with its shafts cocked up in the air, became embedded in a thick thorn hedge! Charlie soon crawled out of the dry ditch, for it was summer-time, and when it was obvious that there were no injuries, the assistant could not stop roaring with laughter! Charlie wasn't amused! Now the bags did have to be unloaded, but eventually men and float were on the road again. If an incident such as this should happen on that bridge today, it would without a doubt cause a major accident, for the main road which passes the lane over the bridge, is now a busy trunk road!

However the partridge chicks did eventually get their

proteins, Charlie got a bad scare, and so, evidently, did Blazes. A couple of years later whilst on a similar expedition after bags of soil, as the headkeeper called them, the horse refused to go over the bridge, even though she was approaching it from the opposite direction with an empty float. No amount of leading and coaxing could make the mare face that bridge again, and quite a long detour had to be made to a modern bridge with a much smaller hump! Elephants may never forget, but it seems as if horses never forget either.

Gamekeepers and poachers, the words go together like 'bread and cheese', but without the same compatability. Poachers are the bane of a keeper's life, and where game is abundant it is seldom that poachers are not. Times have changed and so have poaching methods, but only to a degree. The old time poacher lacked the transport of his modern counterpart, and this naturally restricted his activities to a comparatively small radius. Maybe a few miles from home was the limit, beyond that it became increasingly difficult to avoid the keepers and the police, so many of the old timers only 'worked' close to home. When they used cycles to travel to a good hunting ground, their chances of being caught became that much greater, for you can't melt into the shadows when riding a bike!

Yes, the poacher of today, and of yesteryear, needs now and needed then a certain amount of skill or maybe cunning would be a more suitable word. Some of them would perhaps like to call themselves craftsmen for they certainly did little other than poach!

Rabbits were inevitably the main quarry in those pre-myxomatosis days when they infested the countryside in vast numbers. Pheasants and partridges were also taken by these men of the night, and for each quarry a different technique was needed. By and large most of the rabbits were caught in long nets, as I have described earlier. These were usually fifty yards long and about a yard deep, and when they were run out and pegged up, under the right conditions, and in a place abounding in rabbits, the haul could be amazing. In those days before the war, three or four nets set in one long line could easily yield as many as eighty, ninety or even a hundred rabbits. Thus for

poachers it was a very popular means of taking rabbits. Even in those days a poacher could get six pence, old money, for a nice clean rabbit, and netted ones always are nice and clean. Now a couple of nights' netting could bring as much, if not more in the way of cash, than a week's wages so it is no wonder that there were always poachers around.

The keepers did not mind the locals taking the odd rabbit, it was an accepted practice, but men coming at night, that was a different kettle of fish. Many things were done to ensure that poaching was none too profitable. Thorn boughs cut from adjacent bushes would be strewn indiscriminately on the outside of a wood. A long net run out on top of such a bough would be little use for the rest of the night, and only daylight would enable the entangled mesh to be freed, when indeed in many cases repairs would be needed. When no thorn boughs were to hand, short lengths of barbed wire served the same purpose, in fact, if anything, they were more effective. The wire also had the advantage that it could easily be removed at dusk, if the keeper needed to net that particular patch. Another ruse employed by the keepers was to put a peg in the ground some distance out in the field, run a thin wire from it over a bough of a tree in the wood, and tie a couple of tins on the end with a pebble in each. This only needed to be touched by poachers setting a net for the pebbles to create a din. It had its drawbacks, for if cattle were in the field, the tins would rattle a number of times during the night. At least that tended to make the rabbits stay in the safety of the wood, but it did not inform any keeper in the area whether poachers were afoot.

Where the poaching of rabbits or for that matter pheasants, was very prevalent, it was not unusual for alarm guns to be set. These guns are perfectly harmless, and quite legal, in fact a modern version of them can be bought today. The old version consisted of a rod with a block of metal on it that was near ground level when the rod was pushed in the ground. This block was drilled to take a blank cartridge, on top of which was placed a cap, with a striker to fire the cartridge. At the top of the rod, a sliding weight was held up by a trigger mechanism to which was attached a thin, usually brass trip wire. One end of this was attached to the trigger, then run out at about knee height, across a ride in a wood, or on the outskirts. It had to be knee high so that the gun would not be set off by a prowling badger, but a human interloper would walk into it unsuspectingly in the dark of the night.

This gun has been most useful in the past, warning many a keeper that poachers were afoot. However, the modern poacher, who mainly goes after pheasants does not mind using a torch, and is thus able to pick out the tell-tale wire and avoid it. The old timers never used a light of any description, for fear that it would give away their presence, which of course it would, but the modern day stealer of game has no such qualms. Frequently poachers are dropped off at suitable spots by a vehicle which is only stationary for a few moments, then without wasting any time they will go through a covert, using a high-powered torch to pick out the roosting pheasants. Using powerful air rifles or even .22 rifles, they soon have as many birds as they can carry, and are away to a pick-up point. There, at a pre-arranged time, a vehicle not necessarily the one that dropped them off, will arrive, and stopping only for a second or two for the gang to load up, it is away. This makes the gamekeeper's task difficult indeed, but evidence of a nocturnal visit is always left behind and although it may be some time before that particular gang puts in another appearance, plans can be made to deal with it.

Partridges are not as numerous as in the days of chemical-less husbandry, and it is doubtful if there is much poaching of these lovely little brown birds. It took quite a lot of skill, a lot of local knowledge and the right sort of night to obtain a successful haul. It was essential for the would-be poacher to know where the partridges were 'jugging' that particular night, and it was an indication to the keeper that something might be afoot, if a person, and not necessarily a stranger, was to be seen lurking around the area where partridge were accustomed to roost. On one occasion a poacher even went to the trouble of climbing a telegraph pole, so that he had a wider view. Using climbing irons to assist him, he drew little attention

from passers by, who took him to be a Post Office employee. A keeper spotted him from a distance, and after keeping watch through his binoculars, came to the conclusion that no repair work was being carried out.

It was September, and partridges were in season, so the keeper, being suspicious as are most keepers, laid on a night watching party. Three keepers were out, and keeping watch over an area around that telegraph pole. Sure enough, a couple of hours after darkness had fallen, the keepers could hear the whirr of partridge wings, as a covey took off into the blackness of the night. This was the sign they had waited for, and as they converged on the point where the partridges had risen, one keeper came face to face with two men, laboriously drawing a partridge drag net across the uneven field. The poachers did not even attempt to escape by running away, being loth no doubt, to leave their precious net.

When the other watching keepers arrived it was found that a number of little brown birds had already been taken, probably from some distant field, as the birds were almost cold. Of course the net and birds were confiscated and the two men eventually appeared before the local magistrate.

Now a partridge net is quite a large affair, maybe eighty yards by five yards, with a strong hauling line along one of the five-yard edges. The line would extend several yards either side of the net, which could be dragged across a field by hauling in the lines. If poachers heard the sound of rising partridges, the net was immediately dropped, in the hope that it had enmeshed the birds as they left the ground. It was a rather hit or miss affair, even when you knew where partridge had jugged down for the night. This sort of net took some time to knit, and the amount of twine needed was considerable, so most poachers were loth to abandon this tool of their 'trade'.

There were, and for that matter, still are, many more poaching methods, and things poached. Hares, although not in very great demand, are sometimes the object of the poacher's attention, maybe at times purely for the sport of it. Very often dogs are used, and they come in various breeds and sizes, from a true greyhound to a Jack Russel terrier! As a rule the smaller dogs are used to flush the hare

116

from its 'seat' and the larger ones then course it, but the number killed is not more than one in eight or nine, so this type of poaching must really be purely for sport. When a poacher really wants a hare, the usual method is to use a 'gate net'. This is a stronger version of the long rabbit net, but only five or six yards in length and thus easily concealed in a large pocket. After surveying the area in which he has decided to operate, the poacher would set his net across a suitable gateway. When they leave a field, hares have a habit of making for a gate or a large gap in a hedge, and the poacher will make use of this trait. Having set the net, not too taut and not too slack, he will make a detour round the perimeter of the field. On reaching the far side, he will walk the field in the direction of the set net and the odds are that any hares that jump up will make for the gate, and become entangled in the mesh of the net.

One laddie out on one such expedition after a hare, had rather a shock. He arrived at the spot he had decided to set his net, and glancing round could see no sign of life. The net was set, and off he went to put up a 'puss', but what he didn't know was that he had been seen by a gamekeeper as he emerged from a deep ditch, where he had been 'doing a job for himself'. The keeper immediately spotted what was going on and sneaking along the ditch managed to get to the gate net without being seen. Sure enough it wasn't long before a hare, with its long loping strides appeared and ran straight into the net, where it started to squeal with that ear piercing noise almost like a child in trouble. The poacher picked up speed and as he bent down to remove his captive from the net the keeper bobbed up and put the fear of the Lord into the unsuspecting man. It was a lucky and easy apprehension of an unwanted visitor.

This chapter has by no means covered all aspects of poaching for I have not enough knowledge or experience of say salmon or deer poaching to write about them. Indeed it is rare for a gamekeeper to have covered all aspects of game rearing and protection, and most keepers are specialists in one or two branches of their art.

8 *The seasonal workers*

Many country folk have always depended on mainly seasonal work for a living and could be relied upon to be available at 'muck spreading', haymaking and harvest. Some lived a settled country life, others were itinerant, but not in the gypsy sense. All of these folk were important in their own way although this was not always appreciated by regular workers.

The smaller farms or small holdings in particular, were often not large enough to warrant a full-time employee and they were always glad of this casual labour at haymaking or maybe later in the year at 'tater' picking time. Many small holdings could not rely on one particular crop or on milking alone and so there could well be much seasonal work for the casual labourer. These men had to have a variety of skills, although they were basically required to do the heavier type of work, such as loading manure on to a cart from the winter midden. Now this may seem a straightforward job, and in a way it is, but skill really proves essential when a man may be doing this for ten

118

hours or so with only short breaks. The material to be moved has to be 'weighed' up and once the direction it is lying has been sorted out, it can be lifted into the cart. Now this has to be done with a smooth rhythmic motion, there must be no tugging to pull the material free. Once the fork is clear, it must swing up to the cart at the correct angle and speed so that its load slides off into the cart and the fork is on its way back to repeat the process almost before the material settles in the vehicle.

Many Irishmen came over in the old days to work on the farms, and they would move from place to place. Most were provided with accommodation in the farm buildings, and the larger establishments had a 'bothy' where two or three men would live during the busy season. As a rule these men went back to their native country during the winter months, but usually returned the following year, frequently getting work on the same farm year after year. The odd one would take up permanent residence if he found a suitable job. There are still one or two such men around but with modern machinery the manual labourer is no longer needed and the spring influx of men seeking work no longer takes place.

One Irishman who took up residence in rural Cheshire soon became popular, for, apart from being a good worker, he had a remarkable Irish wit, of which he was mostly unaware! This chappie has been retired for some time now, and still pays his weekly visit to the local pub for a drop of 'Liffey water' as he says. For many years several locals met one night a week to play the 'spots' (dominoes) and of course as the years passed the number dwindled until there were only Paddy and Alf left. The pair kept up the tradition, and still had their weekly game until age caught up with Alf who had to stop visiting the pub and eventually took to his bed. Now Paddy could no longer have his game of 'spots', for the younger generation were not interested. However the son of one of his former companions who called one evening to see old friends, took pity on Paddy and had a couple of games with him. This happened several times over a period of two or three months, for Paddy could be relied upon to be in his usual corner on his weekly visit to the pub. Each time Joe, the son of Paddy's former companion, asked about Alf's health, but there was no sign of any improvement, which was not unexpected as Alf was well into his eighties.

At last the inevitable happened, Alf died. A couple of weeks or so after the last of Paddy's domino-playing friends departed this earth, Joe once again called at the pub, and could tell at once from Paddy's face that something had happened. After the usual greetings Joe said, 'What's up Paddy, you look as if you have lost a quid and only found a tanner.' 'Aye now, for sure,' says Paddy, 'It's worse than that, poor old Alf's gone "jed on us".' There was a pause, but of course Joe was not really surprised at the news, only that he hadn't heard sooner. 'Oh aye' he says, 'and when did this happen Paddy?' 'Well' said Paddy 'I'm not rightly certain how long 'tis'. Then there was a long pause whilst Paddy tried to reckon up the days. At last he said, 'Now it's a fact, if poor old Alf had lived 'till Friday, he'd have been dead a fortnight.'

The Welsh Dee valley is, or perhaps it should be said was, famous for its strawberry growing, for the climate and soil were ideal for the production of this luscious crop Strawberry growing is a labour intensive job, and that is probably why fewer are grown than in the past. Every summer literally hundreds of folk would invade the valley in search of work, 'strawberry dodging' as it was called. How the word dodging came into it is anyone's guess, for the jobs they were seeking entailed picking the plump red fruits!

Bellis Brothers, growers of strawberries in large quantities in the old days, had large huts, probably ex-army huts which were used to accommodate the influx of labourers They had to work long hours in the fields, and no doubt were sick of the smell of strawberries, let alone the taste of them long before the picking season came to an end.

As is often the case when a number of casual labourers get together there was much merry-making in the evenings, and for that matter on wet days when the strawberries could not be picked, for they soon rot if picked when wet. The presence of these folk certainly brought a normally quiet village to life and of course meant a welcome improvement in trade for the local shopkeepers. No

120

much skill was needed to gather a basket of strawberries, but speed was essential to these labourers. It was common practice to pay by results, so the more baskets or punnets that were filled the greater the income for the picker. The experienced 'dodger' would often only pick the largest or larger fruit, and thus fill a basket more quickly. This of course suited the growers, for a basket of large berries is always more attractive and frequently will bring a better price. As the season progressed, and it is only a short one, lasting a few weeks, the strawberries became smaller and smaller, and towards the end of the season, the fruit would go for jam making. After the last gathering of fruit to be sold, the local folks would be allowed on to the field to see if they could get enough fruit to make a few jars of jam, and of course they all did.

Today strawberries are rarely gathered to be sold 'at the gate', and casual labourers are rarely seen. *Pick your Own* notices abound wherever strawberries are grown, and this applies to many other fruits as well. Yes, you may pick your own all right, but that doesn't mean it's free. You have your gathering weighed on your way out, and then dip into your pocket to pay! This must make the operation viable, and no doubt in many cases shows a handsome return. When motor cars were first used by those rather better off than the average working man, it was said that you could tell what sort of strawberry season it had been by the number of new cars in a certain village. This was perhaps envy on the part of some people, but it was quite true, for it was noticeable how many strawberry growers either bought new cars or changed their old ones around midsummer, when the strawberry season was over!

Now and again one or two 'strawberry dodgers' would stay behind when the season was over, and not go on as most of them did for the hop picking. It could not have been easy for them to eke out a living and quite a few of them lived rough, spending their nights in hay lofts, or sometimes, in hovels. These hovels, which were dotted about the countryside made a handy place for a night's sleep. Most of them had a store of hay for the winter feeding of young stock, and so it was possible to be snug and warm even on a cold night.

One dodger had been around for a number of years and spent most nights, summer and winter, in one of these hovels. The farmer knew all about Evan, in fact would give the old lad a feed now and again. As the months went past he became well known in the district, and got the odd job on the farms, even if only for an hour now and again. This gave him enough cash to pay for his meagre needs and a pint or two of ale in the local pub.

In the winter Evan would wend his way 'home' to 'Snow Ball Mansion' as he called the hovel, taking the same track across the fields each night. The gamekeepers, when out night watching, knew his time and route, so kept out of his way, not wishing to frighten the old lad. This was all well and good, but one summer morning a keeper was passing Snow Ball Mansion, and noticed that the door was open. It was a normal door not the split stable type. 'Not like Evan', thought Jim, for Evan was very careful to shut all gates, or leave them as he found them as he moved around the countryside. Jim closed the door, and as there were young cattle in the field, wedged the latch so it could not be opened easily, not wishing them to get at the hay within, let alone Evan's 'bedding'. Nearly two days passed before Jim went that way again, but as he approached the hovel he thought he could hear noises within. Sure enough when he got closer he was certain someone was trying to open the door. When he had taken the wedge from the latch and flung the door wide, who should tumble out but Evan. He was in a rather worse state than his normal bedraggled one, but still quite cheerful, and he said to Jim, 'Wish Old "Pop" (the farmer) had looked in, for 'ee shut door. I've no watter left'. Jim didn't say that he had fastened the door, but he gave him a shilling, telling him to make his way to the nearest pub and get some bread and cheese! A shilling would buy a feed in those days.

It was quite natural for Jim to fasten the door, for he thought that at that time of day Evan would be sure to be on his rounds. But it was really a godsend that he passed that way again, thereby probably saving Evan's life. The old lad spent many more nights in his 'Mansion' and several years later was found by a farmer one morning, lying in the 'bing' in a shippen. Evan had pneumonia, and after only a couple of days in hospital, passed away. He was buried locally, after farmers and friends had made a collection so that the poor soul did not go in a pauper's grave.

If Evan didn't have many skills at least he had the skill to survive under what were at the very least, most uncomfortable conditions, and he must have suffered many hardships over the years. Despite this he was a cheerful character, and with his passing, another facet of country life went too.

Quite a few men did not have regular jobs and for that matter did not wish for one, since they could eke out a living doing odd jobs here and there. Often there would be an acre or so of land to their cottage, which would enable them to keep a milking cow. This would often be tethered by the roadside during spring and summer to graze on the grass verges, for in some country areas these are quite wide. This would enable them to take a crop of hay off their own land for feed in the winter. The milk would produce butter, and even the buttermilk would make a good feed. It was said that many a country child was reared on 'Tatties and buttermilk', at least it was a wholesome feed!

'Am' (Ambrose) was one of those who could not bear to be tied to one job. In fact he was known to pack a task up when he was bored with it. He could not be called idle by any means, for over a period of many years he was the grave digger at a church some three miles from where he lived. Now a six-foot-deep grave takes quite a bit of digging, especially in the heavy clay ground in this particular area, and as the years passed it became rather a burden to Am, for by the nature of things there was only limited time to get the grave dug. Eventually Am had no option but to tell the Vicar he could no longer carry on. The Vicar was naturally very concerned about this, for men to take over such a job could not easily be found. 'Now Am,' said the reverend gentleman, 'If I collect you in the car, and take you back when you have completed your task, will you carry on?' Am had complained about his 'screws' (rheumatism) as a result of which he could no longer ride his cycle, so the Vicar thought this offer might solve the problem. 'Nay boss' said Am, 'I canna put you to

123

that trouble.' 'No trouble at all! I'll take you back after the service when you have filled the grave in, we only have two or three a year anyway.' 'Aye I know that,' said Am, 'but its no use I canna do it.' 'Now come on Am, I don't know who else could do the job as well as you,' said the Vicar, soft soaping the old lad. 'All right then,' said Am, 'But you'll have to guarantee me two a week, I could do with the money.' There was no answer to that, and eventually the vicar got a local chap to take over from Am.

Most of these old lads who scratched a living by doing odd jobs and casual labour were fond of a pint of ale and spent most if not every evening in the local hostelry, although where the money came from is anybody's guess. Some were poachers by repute, and no doubt did take the odd rabbit, but to the best of my knowledge I cannot recall one of them ever being caught, and over a long period it is doubtful if they would have been all that lucky.

Am, true to form, was fond of his nightly tipple. Now during the summer months many people would be having picnics by the River Dee, some mile or so from Am's house. Some would come by boat, some on cycles, and even some of the villagers would take a basket of food to sit by the flowing stream. A lot of coarse fishermen also spent the best part of Sunday 'drowning a worm' and a number of them would adjourn to the nearest pub around midday. When they left it was not at all unusual for them to take a bottle or two of beer with them, there was no canned ale in those days. Each bottle would have a penny (old money) deposit on it, but as it might be some weeks before they fished the same place again, most of the empty bottles were left on the river bank.

Am knew all about this and sometimes late on a Sunday evening he would take a stroll along the river, and almost without fail would retrieve a few of the discarded bottles. He knew where to look: a large area of flattened grass might well produce an empty lemonade bottle or two, for the signs showed that children had been playing there. A smaller area of trampled herbage indicated that an angler had spent some time trying to coax a fish to take the dangling bait, so this spot was more likely to yield an empty beer bottle. Some people would even throw an empty bottle into the slow flowing river, and as long as the screw top was in place, (they were all screw-top bottles in those days) the bottle would slowly drift down stream and eventually come to rest on a bend where there was often a sloping sandy bank. Am would look there too, and his leisurely stroll would often produce six or seven bottles. Of course, knowing which bottles the local publican had charged a penny deposit on, he would discard the others.

By the time he had done his rounds there would still be time to call at the pub to produce the bottles and claim the penny on each one. It doesn't sound much today, but with beer only four pence a pint, the old lad would probably have the wherewithal for two. He was asked one day, as he was making his way to the river, where he was going and what he was after. 'I be on me way for a latchlifter' said old Am, which only left the person who had inquired with a very puzzled expression, for he did not understand Am's words. What Am meant was that if he could get something to lift the latch on the pub door, he would be all right, for if he could only find enough bottles to pay for one pint, there was almost sure to be someone in the pub who would take pity on him and buy him another drink or two! Getting a copper or two by this method can hardly be called a craft, but Am was an opportunist to say the least.

In most areas there would be at least one chap who liked to call himself a 'warrener', but in actual fact he was a rabbit catcher. Many years ago the proper warreners had a full time job looking after rabbits in a confined area, by which I mean an area from which the conies, being fenced in could not escape. It was a way of taking a crop, for the fast breeding rabbits had to be reduced in numbers at regular intervals. A warrener's job was without doubt a skilled one, involving a lot of knowledge such as when to feed and when not to, for in the winter months and sometimes even in the summer when drought conditions prevailed, the conies had to be fed to maintain them in peak breeding condition. In suitable weather and the right conditions, rabbits will breed nine or even ten months of the year, so the better the conditions the warrener could maintain, the greater the crop he was able to take from his warren. Most of these men received only a small wage and relied on the bonus they received for each couple of rabbits sold, which was an incentive to get a high yield!

The rabbit catchers worked on a different basis altogether. Some were paid a weekly wage to kill the rabbits on a farm, or maybe even an estate. Others bought the right to take the conies from the farmer or landowner. This method of buying the right would inevitably lead to a lot of wrangling, for it is most difficult to judge the number of rabbits in a given area at any one time, and of course the price depended on the number that could possibly be caught. Not only the number but the type of terrain had to be considered, for rabbits could be caught or rather trapped more effectively in large open burrows than in smaller burrows covered with undergrowth. Rabbits on sandy soil were often not in such good condition as those on a heavier type such as clay land, and would not command the same price.

The degree to which the area was frequented by poachers also had to be taken into account, for many hundreds of rabbits could be taken in a matter of a week or two by night gangs using long nets. There was also the possibility, if there was a large amount of common trespassing in the area, that a fair number or rabbits would be taken out of any traps set in the daytime. It can be seen that as so many factors were involved it was no easy matter for an agreement to be reached on the price to be paid for taking the rabbits, but by and large most farmers and landowners demanded a fair price, for they wanted the rabbit numbers reduced!

Once an agreement had been reached, the rabbit catcher would waste no time, and would soon be busy setting his traps. Trapping rabbits is hard work, or perhaps more correctly was hard work, when our countryside was alive with bunnies. A hefty man could carry about four dozen of the old gin traps, so that was about the limit a man working on his own would use. The actual setting of the traps was fairly straightforward. The wooden pegs usually cut from elder bushes, had to be driven into the ground, a little spade work was often necessary to make the traps fit snugly in the rabbit holes, and when the traps were in position, the whole lot had to be hidden with a sprinkling

126

of fine soil. Some trappers carried a small sieve with them for this purpose, but most, not wishing to have more impedimenta than necessary, would sieve the soil through their hands. It was essential to make sure no small stones were over the jaws or treadle of a trap, for even a stone or flint not as large as a pea, would prevent the jaws closing and allow the rabbit to escape.

All other holes through which the conies could escape had to be securely stopped, and for this purpose crumpled newspaper was frequently used. By pushing crumpled paper down the holes and covering it with several inches of firmed-up soil the trapper made it difficult for a rabbit to scratch its way to freedom. 'I likes to give 'em something to read,' was what one old rabbit catcher said. Once set, the traps had to be looked at morning and night to remove the luckless rabbits, and of course to keep their suffering to as short a period as possible. Normally the traps were left in the same burrow or burrows for a week, after which they would be moved on to the next set. In some circumstances it was advisable to be in the area as much as possible for it often happened that when a rabbit was caught in a trap its squeal could be heard a long way away. Any person recognizing the sound could easily remove the coney and have a free meal.

One old rabbit catcher, no longer as nimble as he used to be, saw a stranger go to some traps the old lad had set, and walk away carrying a rabbit, as large as life. When old 'Wreaf' got to the trap he was most surprised to find a shilling in the jaws of the trap, in payment for the rabbit that had been removed. Wreaf Close was a good rabbit catcher, having been at it for many years, but it was the first time such a thing had happened to him. Rabbits had often been taken, but no money had been left behind. He said to a crony, 'I wish that fella would go round all the traps and leave a bob in each, it would be easier for me, and pay better.' Rabbits were about ten pence (old money of course) at the time.

The rabbit catcher would almost certainly have set snares at the same time as the traps, and quite likely a hundred snares would catch more rabbits than the forty-eight traps. The snares were mostly set where it was

127

not so practical to set traps, such as in very rough areas and on the outside of woods where many rabbits would be lying out. Ferrets were sometimes used, but this method of getting rabbits is time consuming and not always very productive, for a lot can depend on whether the rabbits are in a bolting mood. Frequently the burrows have to be trapped afterwards to reduce the numbers to an acceptable level.

Sometimes a friend would go along with the rabbit catcher, long netting with him at night, for given the right conditions such an expedition could produce quite a large bag. It would of course ensure that other night prowlers did not cream off a number of rabbits for which the rabbit catcher had paid or would have to pay. Even if they were working on a basis of so much per couple, two or three nights of successful long netting could make an appreciable difference to their income.

The job of rabbit catcher, as opposed to that of the warrener, was seasonal, lasting at the most four months in the winter. A warrener would almost certainly be given other tasks during the high summer, such as helping on the home farm, for many hands were needed in the days before mechanisation, but he would be in receipt of a weekly wage and thus had a fair amount of security. The freelance man had to have other arrows to his bow, and many would be mole catchers as well as rabbit catchers.

Now mole catching is akin to rabbit catching but the flesh in this case is of no use. The skins of moles at one time could demand a good price, so long as they were clean and stretched to the required size. The flesh, however, must be practically inedible for I know of nothing that will eat it. A cat will catch a mole and play with it, but once dead the cat will leave it and will walk away almost with disdain. A vixen will occasionally catch a mole and take it to her litter of cubs, but more than once I have seen the mole outside the entrance to the fox earth, untouched.

There does not seem to be so much concern about moles in the fields these days but the little, almost blind, furry animals, are not very popular in gardens, sports grounds and tennis courts. It does not take a pair of them

128

long to make a fine mess of either cultivated ground or well mown turf. As they eat vast quantities of worms every day, and need regular drinks, moles are always busy, and their underground tunnels can run vast distances, sometimes at a considerable depth. It is not unusual for them to tunnel under an asphalt road, and a garden wall means nothing to them.

Mole catchers are not as numerous as they used to be, and it is not really difficult to see why. The greatest proportion of the old timers were self employed men, and few of them relied on mole catching alone for a living, often having a small holding and various seasonal jobs. The method of payment for their services was based on the damage being done by the moles and the acreage over which this damage was occurring. Sometimes a farmer would retain the services of a really skilled man by paying him so much an acre on the whole acreage of the farm. Such a contract, nearly always verbal, would ensure that mole damage was kept under control at all times.

Modern machinery is not as affected by the mole's heaps of soil as the old harvesting implements were. This, together with the cost of paying a man to catch the moles nowadays, has led to a decline in the numbers of these really skilled men. Many councils have pest officers who are called in when moles become a problem on sports grounds and the like. These men normally use different methods from those of the 'real' mole catcher. Instead of trapping the moles they put a quantity of poisoned earthworms in the mole runs. Worms are acquired from various sources, mainly well rotted manure heaps on the farms. They are then dusted with a poison before being put into the runs, and as soon as the ever hungry mole comes along, the worms are eaten, and the mole poisoned.

Trapping moles is a much more skilful business than poisoning them, and really a much more satisfying method, for at least you know how many you have dealt with. There are two main types of traps, the 'barrel' and the 'spring', both of which, set by the right person, are very effective. The old type of barrel traps were made of wood, but today practically all are of lightweight metal, and a double barrel is also available. This is capable of catching two moles with one setting, so long as they are not going the same way along the run! The spring type is less easy to set, but owing to its shape it is often the most suitable to set in an awkward position.

Experienced men rarely set a trap where the moles are working, for having an intimate knowledge of their quarry they know that at least every four hours the mole will have to go for a drink. The nearest water, be it pond, ditch or river, is where the underground burrower will make for, even if it is half a mile or more away. Percy Lloyd, a mole catcher of great experience, once had the task of dealing with moles on a large area of ground that sloped down to water meadows and a brook. I saw him one day walking along this brook probing the ground with a small spade. Being rather curious, for there were no mole workings in the vicinity, when I got up to him I asked him what he was doing. 'Tha goes for a drink, dunna ye. Aye well, my little friends do too and when I finds what road they be using, them's mine.' It turned out he was looking for the main runs where the moles came for water from the high ground. He did eventually find four well used main runs in which to set his traps, and after being set for a week, the fresh heaps of soil on the high ground ceased to appear, an indication that the majority of the moles had been caught.

After about a week's trapping, the mole catcher would spread the mole heaps about, either kicking them with his hob nailed boots, or if the heaps were large, using a spade, and thus the farmer could see that he had done the job. It was also the custom to hang the skinned carcases of the moles on any available barbed wire, or thorn hedge, as evidence of a good job done.

Setting a trap in the right place and with as little disturbance of the run as possible leads to success. Great care must be taken to ensure that no light can get through to the run, for despite the fact that a mole has very small eyes, and cannot see too well, it can detect light easly. If light gets in, a mole approaching the trap will spot it and almost certainly bore a new tunnel either under or around the trap. When a trap is removed and found to be full of soil, it is almost definitely because light has got through, or

130

as sometimes happens a mole has just been nipped when a trap has been sprung. Once a trap has been sprung and has failed to hold its victim, that particular mole becomes most difficult to catch. In most cases changing the type of trap is the only chance although, even then the trap needs to be set in a different situation, albeit not too far away.

All mole traps are very efficient if set correctly, and are probably the most humane of any of the traps in use. It is rare indeed for a live mole to be found in a trap. The arms of the spring trap have no teeth but operate in such a way that they cross over and exert great pressure on the mole, causing almost instant death. The modern barrel or double barrel has the same crushing effect as a loop of metal tightens on the victim when the trap is sprung.

Normally the moles' workings are greatly in evidence in spring and autumn. During the summer months when the ground is much drier the moles are foraging for food at a considerable depth. When the ground becomes wet the worms come much nearer the surface and then the moles make their tunnels at that level, pushing the soil to the surface as they go. When gardens and sports grounds are watered during dry weather this has the same effect as the autumn rains, and if there are moles in the area, they are sure to find this moist patch of rich soil. So moles are blamed when rows of cultivated seedlings are lifted even though man has made the conditions right!

Moles do come on the surface now and again. They can sometimes be seen crossing the road at night, but they much prefer to be below ground, and it is amazing how fast they can travel. They have to move pretty fast since they often have to go such long distances for a drink, but besides this, it is wonderful to see them go below the surface, if they are caught on the top. On the rare occasion that a mole is caught alive, if it is dropped on the ground, it will just disappear in a matter of seconds. It uses its powerful spade-like front feet to dive below ground, and in no time at all only a very small hole can be seen. It is truly an animal that is more at home in the darkness of the earth than in the light and sunshine.

This reminds me of the supposedly true story of a rural parson and a travelling Irishman. There were many of these Irishmen on the roads in the old days, often making their way back to Liverpool or Holyhead to get the ferry to the Emerald Isle. Although they probably had a pocket full of money after their summer labours on the land, they would nevertheless get as many free meals as they could calling on any likely looking houses. They would of course offer to do a few chores in exchange for a feed, maybe chopping a few 'starting sticks' or brushing up the fallen leaves of autumn. This particular Irishman called at a vicarage, and when the door was opened by the vicar himself he said straight away how hungry he was. 'Now Father, I'm sure a man of the cloth would not turn a poor starving Irishman away without a crust.' 'Indeed not,' said the vicar, 'Come in my good man, you shall have sustenance to see you on your way.' Soon a steaming mug of tea was in front of the Irishman, followed by a heaped plate of bread and cheese with a jar of pickled onions by its side. Of course the vicar talked to his unexpected guest about various country matters, knowing full well that his visitor had spent the season working on the land. 'It's been a poor season zur, now for sure it has,' said the Irishman. 'The harvest has been light and there has been little call for us "casuals". It will mostly be tatties for the family this winter.' Of course the vicar listened to the man's tale of woe, but at the same time he knew that he would have quite a bit of cash in his pockets, and had probably sent a substantial sum back home during the summer. However in his position as the religious leader of the area he felt it his duty to help the man on his way, and offered to pack him a sandwich or two to see him through the day. Just what Paddy was hoping! It would save another call to beg for a feed, and he could stop and have a pint or two of his favourite tipple before finding a hay-filled barn for the night.

The parcel of food was produced, and sticking to the usual routine, Paddy asked, 'Is there any small job I could be doing for ye zur?' Now as the vicarage was next to some lush meadows, for a number of years the lawns had been almost ruined by moles tunnelling in search of worms and pushing up their unsightly mounds. Not really expecting Paddy to do anything about it and probably hoping for the departure of his unexpected guest, the vicar said, 'Do you by any chance know anything about moles?' 'Now for sure I do. You be talking to the right man, father,' said Paddy. 'Could you do something about the little varmints ruining my lawn, and perhaps you could level those unsightly heaps?' 'I'll catch 'em for you Father, you'll be having no more trouble for sure,' said Paddy. 'That's excellent my man, but there is just one thing. As a man of the cloth I should not say this, but they have given me so much trouble, I wonder if you can make them suffer?' 'Now for sure I can,' said Paddy, 'You'll be leaving the whole matter to me.'

Off went Paddy without asking for any traps or a spade, and he could soon be seen kicking the mole heaps on the lawn in all directions. After a while he disappeared and the vicar watching through his study window thought that was the last he would see of the Irishman. But no, half an hour later Paddy came up the path and knocked on the door. Having no option but to open the door and confront the Irishman with soil covered boots, the vicar said 'What now my man?' 'Well I thought you would like to know you would have no more trouble with them mole varmints.' 'Oh yes,' said the vicar, 'And what have you done with them, did you make them suffer?' 'Well now I did for sure' said Paddy, 'I buried them alive!!' and he turned round and walked away without even a smile on his face. Of course the vicar saw the amusing side of it and no doubt the story was told many times and in many places, as I have told it now!

The rabbit catchers and for that matter the mole catchers too, were, despite what is so often said about country folk, pretty wily and crafty, and of course had a tremendous knowledge of the countryside and its mammals. Part of their income depended on the presence of rabbits and moles, for few farmers would want their labours if only a small number of heaps were appearing on the land, and only the odd rabbit could be seen grazing on the pastures. This in a way caused the trappers to use devious means to ensure that their talents would be needed in the future. In a way it was easier for the mole catcher to achieve his ends than the rabbit catcher, even though rabbits breed pretty fast.

As I have said, it was the custom for the skinned carcases of the moles to be hung in a prominent position so that the job could be seen to have been done. Naturally there were more moles in some areas than others, and therefore more carcases were hung up for all to see. But it was essential that where the density of the mole population was not so great, a fair number of carcases should be hung on barbed wire or a thorn bush. Thus it was not uncommon for a crafty mole catcher to take the remains of a mole from one place to another, and give the impression that the mole population had been greatly reduced! This trick would leave enough breeding moles to ensure that the mole catcher's services would be in demand another year. Another way of ensuring that there were enough moles to breed, was to leave them alone until the dry weather, when the furry animals pushed fewer heaps up, for they had to feed on the worms at some depth. The trapper would use his knowledge of this behaviour to his advantage, and if he chose to, would make an excuse of being unable to 'get to them there moles for a week or two'. By the time he got there, the drier weather had arrived, usually in March. He would then set a few traps, catch one or two, maybe bring a carcase or so from a distant place, and after a few days, kick the heaps of soil that the moles had put up, until little sign of any working could be seen.

Some might say this was getting money under false pretences, and perhaps it was, to a certain extent, but at the same time the mole catcher would ensure that no heaps were left to cause damage to any farm machinery. Of course in most cases the farmers knew full well what was going on but accepted the situation, for there was probably a greater spirit of mutual help in bygone days, and the mole catcher had to make a living!

As far as I know mole skins are not in demand these days, man-made fibres have taken over, but at one time quite a part of a mole catcher's income came from the sale of mole skins. There is evidence that the skins are now of little value, for in some places the mole, still with its jacket on, can be seen hung or tied on wire fencing. When there was a demand for the skin with its fine velvet-like fur, the old timer would skin the animal as he walked from one trap to another. I once asked Arthur Thomas, a mole catcher of some repute, why he did this, and he said, 'It be like this. We'em all got a smell and moles have a good nose, but I reckons messing about with a dead 'un, makes it so the little devils can smell mole and not me.' He knew without a doubt for he could certainly catch 'the little devils'. A good clean skin, with its winter 'jacket' would fetch the princely sum of fourpence or fourpence half-penny (old money of course), but if a man caught only a hundred a week (and a good man could exceed that), this represented quite a sum when a labourer's wages were under two pounds a week.

The skins had to be stretched into squares measuring not much less than four and a half inches, by four and a half inches. They were tacked onto either boards or the sides of wooden sheds, in a position where air could circulate freely. After a week or so they were sufficiently dried to be removed, and stored in a dry place until enough had accumulated to be sent off to the fur merchant. The local plumber would also have one or two skins from the mole catcher, for in the days when most pipes were lead, moleskin was the ideal material to 'wipe' a joint, that is to smooth the solder when joining pipes or repairing a burst. Of course the plumber usually got the poorer quality skins!

These mole catchers were great men and despite some of the crafty moves described, they were as honest as the day is long, and nearly always friendly with the game-keepers who of course they could help at times. Many of them were observant naturalists. They are a dying breed unfortunately, for many of the moles caught today are caught by people who can only really be described as amateurs!

9 *Gardeners of the Estate*

It would be wrong for me to write about the skills of so many country dwellers without saying something about the gardeners. Now I am not referring to the cottagers who had large gardens and looked after them so well, but rather to the professional men who worked at the large country houses. Some large houses would employ many such men, for instance Eaton Hall at Chester, the seat of the Duke of Westminster, employed thirty-four gardeners in prewar days. Perhaps that is not quite correct, for around fourteen of them were apprentices who would serve their time at Eaton, under the watchful eye of the head gardener of that time, a Mr Barnes. After five years they would move on, many of them eventually becoming responsible for large gardens and public parks. They would live in a communal house or bothy, with a local lady to come in and clean, but nearly always these lads had to look after themselves when it came to preparing their food. Some might say that they had a hard rough life, but it was without doubt a great character builder and gave them a sense not only of independence but of responsibility too. Today of course the wages for such a large staff would be enormous, but once again, mechanical aids have reduced the labour involved in maintaining a garden. As for growing vegetables, it is cheaper to buy them than pay the wages of one or maybe two men.

At one time a large country house would have had many acres of pleasure garden, anything up to an acre of glasshouses, as well as an extensive area given over to vegetables. The pleasure gardens, many of them laid out originally by that famous landscape gardener Capability Brown, needed constant attention to keep them in prime condition. This alone would tie up quite a number of men. The onset of spring meant the lawn mowers had to come out, and they would be in continuous use until late September. All the walks had to be edged regularly, and of course weeds on these gravel walks could not be allowed to grow. There were no weed-killers as we know them today, so the gravel was kept loose to prevent the germination of the weed seeds. Usually on a Saturday morning unless it was very wet, up to half a dozen of the garden staff would 'scuffle' the gravel, using what is now called a Dutch hoe. As this job was undertaken regularly, the gravel was loose, and even if there was a mile or so of walks, as at Eaton, the task was soon completed. At certain times the gravel would be raked even and level, particularly if the owner of the property was due to take up residence, or if the grounds were going to be open to the public.

The mowing and scuffling must have been boring jobs, but there were also many hedges, mainly of yew, numerous flowering shrubs and herbaceous borders that needed regular attention and perhaps they broke the monotony. The autumn would bring the fall of the leaves of varied hue, and these had to be gathered and carried away. Raked into heaps and then carted to a special spot, they were allowed to rot down and eventually produce that precious commodity in any garden, good leaf mould.

The men who worked in the pleasure gardens were in the main, qualified gardeners, and the results of their endless labours were a delight to behold. At any time of the year there would be colour; in the spring rank upon

137

rank of glorious daffodils which appeared to have been planted haphazardly, although really much thought had gone into the scheme. The various shades and varieties of that carpet of gold had been planted in such a fashion that they blended perfectly. Many generations would see the beauty of such a vast area of spring blossom, for every year thousands more bulbs would be planted, to replace the deteriorating plantings of earlier years. Later bluebells would spring up, and here and there, as the sun filtered through the trees, a sea of azure blue would be seen. Many of the walks had literally thousands of crocus at their edge and what a blaze of colour that made to herald the arrival of spring.

The greenhouses produced everything from very early strawberries through a range of flowers and pot plants to very rare orchids. These houses needed really skilled men to work them for many factors such as temperature, humidity and air flow had to be accurate in order to get good results. Not only had all those factors to be controlled, but the timing of the planting and sowing had to be organised so that many of the pot plants would be at their best to coincide with some annual event in the big house. Yes, it took a lot of skill and dedication to produce exotic blooms completely out of season under conditions very different from those of today. The vast greenhouses, for instance, were heated by hot water. After being heated at a central point, the boiler house, the water was circulated underground from glass pavilion to glass pavilion where large cast iron pipes ran along the inside of the buildings. Some were cool houses and had fewer pipes, but others, the hot houses, had several pipes running along each side. It was not just a simple matter of keeping the boiler going, it must have been most difficult to maintain an even temperature. Today, no matter what the source of heat, there is always a thermostat to adjust to the required setting, and there are also gadgets that open and shut windows or 'lights' as they are called, when the temperature reaches a certain level. It is no longer necessary to watch thermometers continually nor to make frequent adjustments to the light, in the roof of the greenhouse.

At Eaton Hall, and no doubt at many other large houses, there was an orchid house, a greenhouse given over entirely to the production of orchids. This was the domain of one or two skilled gardeners and only the head gardener was allowed in without asking permission. Even the owner, the second Duke of Westminster, would say, 'May I come in?', before entering to inspect the precious plants, many of which were not only delicate but rare. All the year round, many blooms were available for the decoration not only of the Hall itself but also for use in London, at the town house. These when required, would be packed in special boxes, mostly in cotton wool, and put on the London train, where a member of staff from the London household would collect them.

The gardening department was at all times a hive of activity. The men were under the control of the Head Gardener, who of course was a well-respected man with a vast amount of knowledge in all departments. His sole task was to ensure an immaculate garden, and an adequate supply not only of decorative flowers, but fruit and vegetables at all times. Several foremen were required to control each section of the staff of thirty-four in their day to day work, but the Head Gardener gave the orders! It was inevitable that some men were more skilled than others, for instance 'Budder' Jones. 'Budder' may sound a queer nick name, but the old lad acquired it from his one great skill, that of budding roses! Various other plants were propagated by the budding method of course, but roses in particular were needed in large quantities, and it was always the old lad who selected the bushes from which to take the buds.

Perhaps a brief description of propagation by budding would be useful. It is usually done in July and August, but briar 'stocks' must first be available. When needed in large numbers they would be grown over a period of time. The seeds in the hips, or seed pods of the wild or dog rose would be sown, and the seedlings would be grown on to the required size. Some would even be allowed to grow on for a number of years to be used eventually to produce 'standard' roses. By standard I mean roses that have a crown of flowers on one stem, two, three or four feet high.

The budder's job was to take a plump bud from the base of a leaf, at the same time ensuring that a slither of mature wood held the bud. This was trimmed making sure no feathery edges were left and then inserted in a V-shaped cut at a selected point on the stock. This was then bound together tightly with raffia to ensure that all air was excluded from the exposed bark. The bud itself had to be left exposed for it was from this point that growth would take place. All the foliage and weak shoots on the mother stock had to be removed, and this, at least in theory, sent all the sap to the implanted bud, which in due course took hold and grew. I hope thus described it appears comparatively easy, which it is, but the success rate achieved by the average person would probably be less than fifty per cent. Even a professional gardener would be happy with an eighty per cent success rate, so the old lad always got the job of budding, and the nickname to go with it!

There is of course another way of producing rose bushes, that of taking cuttings, a method which can be applied to many other plants. It is a comparatively simple method in which a slip of the parent plant is inserted into the correct compost or soil, where in due course it roots and grows eventually into a replica of the parent. This can be a rather slow process in some cases, for it takes a considerable while for the new plant to reach a decent size, and this is true of rose cuttings. When budded on to a briar stock a reasonable bush is achieved in half the time. Thus at one time budding was the usual method of reproducing a rose. There were disadvantages, however, in using a briar stock for in the course of a few years, the briar would send up suckers, shoots from the briar roots, which eventually reduce the rose growth and make the bush useless. Practically all rose plants bought at garden centres and nurseries have been budded, which I suppose makes commercial sense, for a rose grown from a cutting never throws up suckers and lives for many many years. I have a rose called 'Peace' a favourite with many people, which has delighted us with its fragrant blooms summer after summer, for over forty years, and is still quite healthy. It was grown from a cutting without a doubt, and when purchased cost the princely sum of six old pence!

There would be a foreman over the gang who maintained the vast acreage of the pleasure gardens, with its ornamental water-lily covered fish ponds. This foreman was also responsible for feeding the various hued fish. Another foreman was in charge of the hot house and another in charge of the cooler greenhouses, and of course the vegetable garden must not be forgotten. In many cases the vegetables were grown in a walled garden some distance from and often out of sight of the Hall or big house. It was in a way, a small market garden, with a greater variety of subjects grown than in a commercial one. The kitchen gardens at Eaton Hall were in fact in a village almost three miles distant, and the walled area alone enclosed an acre and a half. This was surrounded by a border twenty yards wide, and next to this was an orchard of four or five acres – some kitchen garden! At one stage fourteen gardeners worked full time cultivating and maintaining this area of fruit and vegetable producing ground. No machines of any sort were used, all the digging was done by hand with a garden spade. Every year a certain portion had to be double dug, a time-consuming process, but one which the head gardener then a Mr Barnes insisted upon. He was also responsible for the greenhouses and pleasure gardens at the Hall. Double digging

means taking out a trench the depth of a spade and then the same depth again, and as work progressed the top soil from the next row of digging would be put in the bottom and the soil from the lower trench placed on top. It was essential to have a wide trench to allow room to work, and to allow for the addition of well rotted farmyard manure.

This process was being carried out one day in these very kitchen gardens during the war years, when several Land Army girls were employed. It was usual for the gardeners to have a break mid morning for a cup of tea, for which fifteen minutes were allowed. Now Mr Barnes paid regular visits to the kitchen gardens, usually arriving just before this break at ten o'clock or around ten fifteen, although sometimes he would ring the changes and arrive a couple of minutes before noon, when the staff stopped for lunch. All these visits were no doubt designed to keep them on their toes and dispel any ideas they might have of knocking off early or having a longer mid morning break! On this particular morning Mr Barnes arrived just as the Land Girls and men were leaving their rest room to restart some double digging. He had the odd word with the men and then spotted one of the girls carrying a spade with a blade only half the depth of a normal one. 'Florence, you aren't going to move much soil with that spade are you?' Quick as a flash Florence replied, 'No sir, but a little spade for a little woman, a big 'un for a mon.' Florence was only about four feet three inches! Mr Barnes was taken by surprise but shortly said, 'I'll tell Mr Thomas (the foreman) to get a new one out for you.' Poor Florence was rather flabergasted by this reply, for it meant that the next day she would have a new spade to break in, and breaking in a spade always made work that much harder for a while. Mr Barnes didn't know, although maybe being a country man he had probably realised, that Florence had brought her father's spade. This tool had worn short, thin and sharp, making a full day's digging much less exhausting than a normal, less used spade. Florence was handed the new spade the next day, but she hadn't taken her father's spade home, having hidden it in a safe place. As soon as Mr Barnes departed that morning after his daily visit, off went Florence and swopped the spades!

142

In the walled kitchen garden there were also quite an area of cold greenhouses. These were used to produce vegetables more or less out of season such as dwarf beans, cauliflowers and of course salad crops. The high brick walls at the back of these greenhouses were clothed with peach and nectarine trees, all of which were fan trained. This type of fruit requires a lot of skilled labour, but the end product is oh so delicious. During the winter months pruning had to be done, and in early spring the walls would be covered in one mass of sweet-smelling pink blossom. This blossom had to be thinned and then as the flowers became fully open, it was essential for them to be fertilized. Every winter the keepers on the estate would receive a request for a number of rabbits' tails or preferably the tails of hares. These tails were tied to long bamboo canes, probably a couple of them to each and then when the sun was shining, and there was plenty of pollen on the blooms, the tails would be dabbed on one blossom after another. This process transferred the pollen and fertilized most of the blooms.

After a few weeks it was necessary to thin out the now visibly swelling small peaches. More than one thinning was necessary, for unless the fruit was at least six inches apart it could not swell to its full potential. For the fruit to get that delightful blush-pink colour, the light and sun had to reach it, so often a few leaves had to be removed as well.

On one occasion whilst thinning the second time round, when some of the fruits had reached the size of ping-pong balls, one of the gardeners asked Mr Barnes if he could have some of the thinnings. 'Why my man?' asked the head gardener. 'Well my wife reckons she could make some peach jam from this immature fruit,' replied Joe. 'Yes certainly,' said Mr Barnes, 'Let me have a pot to try when she has made it.' Well it so happened that another gardener had overheard this conversation. Shortly afterwards Joe was called away by the foreman, and an hour or so later, when he got back to the peaches he found only the small ones lying on the ground. 'Well that's a devil,' said Joe to Cyril, who had also been taken off the job. 'I reckon I know where they be,' and he started to gather up a quantity of the small ones. 'Them's no use,' said Joe, 'all stones.'

143

Cyril winked and walked to a raincoat hanging on the greenhouse door. 'Hey Joe, come and hold your apron under here.' Joe went to him and found that one sleeve of the coat was tied tight with raffia and bulging significantly. He held his apron out, Cyril undid the raffia, and a shower of the largest thinned peaches fell into it! 'Tie it up again quick,' said Cyril and proceeded to fill the sleeve with the small useless fruit. Nothing was ever said about that incident, but Mr Barnes did ask some time later what the jam was like, and eventually received a jar!

During the war years a lot of men from the village belonged to the 'Royal Observer Corps which had a post on high ground nearby. These men were allowed time off work to fulfil their duties, according to a rota system. On this particular morning Cyril Perkins had been on duty from six a.m. until 10 a.m., and arrived back in the gardens as the gardeners and the Land Army girls were finishing their mid morning break. He jumped off his bike and rushed up to them, breathless. 'Quick, quick,' he shouted, 'We'll have to hide.' 'What for?' said the gang in chorus. 'It's dangerous, very dangerous,' said Cyril. 'Why?' said the foreman gardener, 'I haven't heard an air-raid warning.' 'No you wont 'ave, but they're everywhere,' said Cyril. 'Who's everywhere?' the gang wanted to know, and Cyril said, 'The Jerries of course.' This statement brought looks of horror and amazement from those gathered round him, who naturally assumed that as he had just come from the Observer Post, Cyril had the latest information. No one moved but no doubt many worried thoughts were going through their heads. After deftly brushing off several questions, Cyril started to laugh. 'They are you know, they are here, at any rate hereabouts, there's one under every bed.'

To return to the greenhouses and the crops grown in them; one house, of considerable size was given over to the production of very early dessert apples and pears. The trees were grown in large pots, and treated in such a manner that they were in bloom weeks before those in the open. A number of varieties of both apple and pear were needed, since the aim of this very specialised method was to have fruit ready long before any from the orchard, and right up to the time the outdoor fruit was ripe. Maybe only half a dozen apples would be left on each tree, for the fruit was drastically thinned once the blossom had set. The end product was an absolutely perfect specimen, which in looks and flavour put that modern variety, Golden Delicious, completely in the shade.

After a number of years these trees, which were effectively dwarfs, had to be replaced, and many of them found their way into the cottage gardens on the estate. Many of them are still thriving today, but sadly the quality of the fruit they produce is not remotely like it was when the tree started its life in a large clay pot. Few of the varieties could be named now, for unless one of the gardeners took a tree to plant in his garden, the name was lost, and it was thought of as just another good eating apple or pear, as the case may be. In the orchard there were top quality trees producing top quality fruit, which ranged from very early plums through to apples and pears that would keep for months. With such large numbers of trees it was inevitable that there was a lot of waste, but as long as the foreman gardener gave permission, the staff were allowed to have some of the windfalls. Even the kitchens at the Hall would not use these damaged fruits, they would only take the best, which had been gathered carefully and were free from bruises or damage.

One day several men were getting a large basket of particularly good, long keeping apples, and one asked the foreman if he could have a bag of those on the ground. 'Certainly,' said the foreman, 'But only the windfalls', then he departed to let the men got on with their job. One of the gardeners, thinking to be clever said, 'I dunna want any damaged 'uns. I'm having a bagful off that tree, some that will last us all winter.' He then produced a hessian bag, an old army sand bag in fact, and after making sure that the foreman was out of sight, proceeded to fill the bag with sound fruit. His mates did not approve of this, and told him so, but no matter, he said 'The old lad (the foreman) won't know,' and tied the neck of the bag tightly. He then took the full bag to the shed where the men kept their bikes, ready for knock off time. The next day when the same gang was again gathering apples, one of his mates said, 'Are you having any more today?' 'No' he said very abruptly 'and you know why.' 'What's up?,' was the reply, 'You got them home all right didn't you?' 'Aye,' he said, 'but they weren't worth carrying. They was all squashed and useless. I reckon one of yee lot hammered 'em in with a spade or something.' Now none of the gang would or could admit it, for it was quite a mystery to them. Eventually they concluded that it must have been the foreman. The old lad must have had his suspicions and kept well out of sight but in a position to see the fruit being gathered and put into the sack. Damaging the prime fruit was his way of showing that he knew what was going on, and probably caused less hassle than a confrontation. Anyway the 'fly' gardener didn't ask for any more 'windfalls'.

Large estates rarely paid high wages in prewar days, for it was normal policy to employ a rather larger staff than was really necessary. The employees were by and large happy, the rent for their cottage was low, a peppercorn rent really, and there were always a fair number of perks. There was a saying in this part of Cheshire that a job on Eaton Estate was a good 'un, for it was 'Thirty four bob a week and plunder!' Of course it wasn't plunder so much as perks.

The household staff would get surplus food, dripping and the likes. The gamekeepers had what rabbits and pigeons they wanted, but no game! The foresters or woodmen had, 'starting sticks', logs, pea and bean sticks, and the gardeners would at various times be allowed to take home damaged or windblown fruit. Naturally at times the temptation to have better quality fruit got the upper hand, and the odd chap would seize an opportunity when it occurred. This rarely met with the approval of his workmates for there was a tradition of honesty and loyalty amongst the staff in all departments.

If one employee got away with taking anything that could not really be classed as a perk, there was always the possibility that others would do the same, and of course eventually a state of distrust would be created. However on the odd occasion that items were taken that shouldn't have been, in other words, stolen, I cannot recall one such case where the police were called in. The loyal staff ensured that such an incident was not repeated.

Mention of the police brings back memories of the old time rural or village bobby. He was of course part of the community and rarely had anything serious to deal with. The gang of boisterous teenagers gathering round the village pump or shop in the evening were soon dispersed with a cuff round the ears from the policeman's gloves. As there were few cars there were no traffic problems. Perhaps a lad coming home late from courting had flooded the carbide in his cycle lamp and was riding without lights. A word of warning from the man in blue made that lad very careful, but at the same time any recurrence could bring the wrath of the law down on the lad and he would probably be fined half a crown (twelve and a half new pence) at the local magistrate's court! Marvellous chaps those policemen were. Their skills were very different from those of the men in the force today. Since they lived in a rural community they had to be countrymen, at least by inclination if they were not born and bred to it, and they had to be fully aware of country goings-on. I knew one such bobby who was keen on all country sports. He nearly always managed to arrange to have his day off when a shoot was taking place, and was often out ferreting with the keepers and farmers. He was of course also aware of the possibility of poaching activities and would contact the keepers should he see or hear anything suspicious during his nights on duty. It was not unusual for him to knock a keeper up around midnight with a tale of having heard something suspicious in a particular wood. Of course the keeper would get up and the pair of them would set off to investigate, and every time there would not be the slightest sign of any poaching activity. When they arrived back at the keeper's house they would always have a cup of tea. When the tea was brewed Alf would want to know if there was anything in the bottom, saying 'I be near frozen, hanging around on a night like this.' Well what Alf wanted was some whiskey in his tea! He would hang on talking to the keeper, probably end up by having a sandwich or two, and then say at about a quarter to two, 'I'll be on my way, I goes off at two.' This sort of incident would occur regularly with different keepers during the winter months, but on most occasions

147

Alf was only after a drink and a warm to help pass his lonely night hours on duty.

It must be said in all fairness that that same policeman would turn out at any time, day or night, to help the keepers when poachers were known to be operating, and he often played a great part in catching the trespassers.

Visiting the farms on his beat was part of the village policeman's duty, for even many years ago there were rules and regulations that the farmers had to adhere to. A policeman had to be present when sheep dipping was taking place for instance, or at least he had to put in an appearance, for his signature would be required on the appropriate document. It didn't take a bobby long to find out where he was welcome, for not all farmers were pleased to see the arm of the law arrive, even if they weren't bending the rules. A cup of tea and a chat often yielded information that was useful to the policeman, and the farmer liked to think he was being looked after by the law. Often the bobby would have a parcel under his cape when he departed on his cycle, maybe a piece of butter or cheese or even a few fresh eggs. His visit was probably made in the hope of this anyway!

Joe, one of these village policemen, has long since retired, and this incident happened many years ago now. It was shortly after personal radios had been issued to all 'men in blue', and many of the rural police officers were driving around in cars. Joe was at a bit of a loose end and found himself in the vicinity of a large farm where he always received a welcome. Sure enough when Joe knocked on the door, the farmer's wife shouted, 'Come on in.' When Joe got into the kitchen, he found another man sitting by the fire, 'How do,' said Joe and sat down in a handy chair. He noted that the stranger had a glass of whiskey in his hand and thought 'I'm in with a chance here.' Sure enough the farmer's wife produced a glass with a liberal dose of the amber liquid. The stranger, who had not been introduced, started talking about various country sports, and remarked that he had called to pick Jim, the farmer, up to take him to a rugby match. Whilst the pair were engaged in conversation Jim's raucous voice blared out, 'Who the hell's come now?' His wife replied, 'It's Joe

148

the bobby.' 'Well give the old B—————— a drop of whisky.' 'He's got some' said his wife. 'Well give him another.' Jim's wife duly carried out his orders and refilled Joe's glass and that of the stranger. Shortly after, Jim appeared in his going out suit. 'We'm be going to a rugby match Joe,' said Jim, 'So tha'd better sup up. I anna leaving yee with the missus. You know yon mon, dinna ye?' he said, pointing to the stranger. 'Hang on' said Joe, 'I'll switch this radio off. They're nowt but a damn nuisance,' and he switched his personal radio off. 'Now what were you saying Jim?' 'I said you know Bill here don't you?' was Jim's reply. 'No never seen him before, not as I can recall,' said a puzzled Joe. 'Well you should know him, he's Chief Constable of —————shire,' (an adjoining county). One can visualize Joe's reaction for he was on duty, in uniform, drinking whiskey, with his radio off!!

Luckily the Chief Constable was an understanding man and said, 'Don't worry Joe, I've done the same thing myself when I was in a lower rank, but I didn't have a radio to turn off.' This eased Joe's worries a bit, but he was still rather apprehensive, in fact it was a month or more before his mind was finally set at rest, when his Superintendent asked him how he liked Mr —————, the Chief Constable of the adjoining force. Joe knew then that his lapse at Jim's farm had not been reported to his senior officer!

Grand chaps these village policemen were, but alas, things have changed. One officer in a car has to cover an area where there used to be two, three or more men on foot and cycles to maintain law and order. Mobility is essential these days for the wrong 'uns are able to cover a large area in pursuit of their unlawful activities. Cars, cars, cars, there are more and more every year and people change them like shirts which does not make it any easier for a beat bobby to know what's what on his patch.

There was a village bobby a few years ago called Bill Mapp who had a wonderful memory for car numbers. I remember once talking to him about various country happenings, when a car went past. Bill looked at it and said, 'Oh aye, I see John S. has changed his car again, the old 'uns number was so and so, the one before that so and so.' He then rattled off a series of car numbers he thought

149

I should remember, for they had been seen parked in unusual places during the hours of darkness, and thus could possibly belong to poachers. Bill could memorise the number and make of any car that he should happen to see whilst on duty, which at times must have proved most useful. This was·in the days before police computers, when a car number took some time to trace, but Bill Mapp had all the information about local cars and many more stored in his brain!

Having known many friendly village policemen over the years I should love to tell a lot more tales, but in many cases it would probably embarrass them if I did so. There was Rex Norbury, my tutor during my early days as a Special Constable; Sergeant Alf Jones, the section sergeant, an understanding and able man; Bill Mapp who has already been mentioned, and Dave Maddox now serving on Bill's old beat who cannot be left out. Dave is a jovial chap always full of the joys of spring. He has a wonderful 'nose' for you can bet that if my wife makes that marvellous concoction 'Tatty cakes', Dave will arrive 'on business'. 'Aye' says I, 'What business? To scoff some of our tatty cakes.' Of course he only laughs and anyway he is very welcome. I wonder some times how he does know what's on the menu, for this delicacy is only made three or four times during the winter months! There was also Ken Roebuck, a dog handler who has retired from the force but now trains dogs and writes books in America. He was one of the best dog handlers I have ever known, and a great help over the years in catching poachers. Then there is Alf Woodcock, a grand old retired Constable, but I have mentioned him before.

Now all these men of the law loved the rural life, and this was essential if they were to do their job properly. It was of course also essential that they were on good terms with most of the folk who worked on the farms and even those who worked on the roads. By the roads, I mean the 'lengthsmen', unfortunately no longer to be seen with their brushes and hooks. These men, employed by the local council, were responsible for keeping the roads and verges tidy, each being responsible for a certain area. Today mobile gangs do this type of maintainance, but in no way do they approach the standard set by the 'lengthsmen'.

There were no weed-killers with which to spray the verges and 'channels' (gutters) so the men had to do all the work by hand. Some villages had cobbled gutters which soon became weed grown after the carted hay had shed so many seeds. A three-cornered hoe, perhaps triangular is a better way to describe the tool, was used to clear the cobbles of weeds, and a time consuming, boring job it must have been. Council roadmen have always had the reputation of leaning on a brush half of the time, but these lengthsmen could not do a lot of that, for as they worked on their own it was possible to see what work had been done each day. Naturally they were not averse to local gossip and would always have a few words with any folk passing, and no doubt passed on any tit bits gleaned from the friendly villagers. Strangers in the area came under extra special scrutiny and at times they could prove helpful to the local bobby who was 'making enquiries'.

Arthur Edwards, who lived until well into his eighties, was a lengthsman most of his life, and of course was well known over a large area. A most conscientious and cheerful man, he was always willing to help where needed. The normal time to start work was seven thirty, but Arthur would always arrive some time before that and ride round the village on his cycle. The reason why he toured his 'patch' was to see which area needed attention first, maybe there had been a dance in the village hall, and a certain amount of litter had gathered in the road. Perhaps a gang of youths had gathered by the shop the previous evening, and left evidence of their larking about. Arthur would note what needed to be done and make it his business to deal with it before setting off to his task for that day. With the onset of autumn Arthur was particularly busy. He could not bear to see corners filled with wind-blown piles of leaves, and his hand cart was filled many times in the course of a day. As he passed the cottages with his hand cart he would stop and gather any leaves which had accumulated inside the gates and along the path. This simple and friendly gesture earned him many a cup of no doubt very welcome tea. The laden hand cart was taken to a nearby wood, and the leaves deposited on a large heap.

Often Arthur could have unloaded the cargo of leaves without pushing the cart so far, but there was a reason why he put all the leaves in one place. Arthur was a dedicated gardener, and come the spring, a passing waggoner would be asked to take sacks of leaf mould to Arthur's house.

When the dedicated worker retired the villagers presented him with a watch as a token of their esteem, at a special social evening.

Another character who spent most of his life keeping the roads, lanes and villages tidy, was Bill Heanor. Made in much the same mould as Arthur, he was a popular figure until his retirement some years ago. Bill had a speciality if it can be called that; swopping plants! In the spring of the year if someone had plenty of sprout plants, but no cabbages he would see Bill and tell him the situation. Sure enough the next day Bill would call with the required cabbage plants. He would then take some of the surplus sprout plants and pass them on to someone who needed them, and perhaps take away with him a bundle of cauliflower plants, and so it went on. The same process applied to summer bedding plants and come October, Bill could be seen with a parcel of wallflower plants on his bike, probably to be swopped for forget-me-nots! I don't think he ever took any home for his own quite considerable garden. Bill lived and still lives in the next village, a village of quite some size, which boasts a chemist, a butcher and hardware shop as opposed to the usual Post Office and general store. Two or three mornings a week Bill could be seen calling at cottages on his patch where old folks lived and he would be delivering small packages. He knew when the doctor had called on any aged folk, and before finishing work for the day he would call and see if there was a prescription which needed collecting. The old folk were of course very grateful, and no doubt the chemist in Bill's village was pleased with the extra business.

The countryside is a worse place for the passing of these roadsmen, for the modern machinery used to cut the verges does not leave a small bird's nest in peace, as Arthur and Bill would, nor does it gather leaves from inside a cottage gate – ah well, that's progress.

10 *Time off*

It is impossible to write about country folk, their characters and their skills, without thinking of their pastimes and
hobbies. Before the days of television, and even of radio,
despite the fact that they worked long and arduous hours,
they did have some time to indulge in hobbies and sports.
The children in particular had time on their hands. It was
rare for the village school to give them any homework, and
as many would have a considerable distance to walk to
their homes, mostly along country lanes, they had an
opportunity for their favourite spring pastime, the collecting of birds' eggs. Many a country lad had a large collection
of eggs, some even of quite rare species, and in a way this
hobby taught them quite a lot about the wildlife and even
the flora of their particular environment. They knew
where to look for certain birds' nests and what type of
herbage or bush a particular bird favoured. They knew the
courting songs of many birds as well as many of their alarm
notes. Over the years the egg collecting hobby has died
out, partly because most wild birds are now protected
(but I don't think that would stop some kids) and partly

because of what is taught in schools. This can only be a good thing. Many factors have taken a toll of our bird population quite apart from the nests being robbed, although many years ago when egg collecting was the hobby of most country lads, it seemed to have little effect on the number of birds around. Children are bussed to school these days, and get a lot of homework, so thankfully everything has combined to give our feathered songsters a chance of survival, at least where schoolchildren are concerned.

Fishing during the summer months took up a lot of the children's spare time. Cheshire is a county with hundreds of ponds or pits, as well as 'meres' (lakes) and a river or two. The children would spend many happy hours dangling a worm, which was often only tied to a piece of string on a bean pole in the clear weed-edged ponds. There was not a large variety of fish to be caught in these waters, but in some of the marl pits, there would be myriads of small rudd. This was grand fun for the kids, and it was amazing how adept they were at hooking these glittering silver fish. They rarely took any home, but often moved them in a battered tin full of water to another pond which had proved less productive. When eels were caught, as they were at certain times of the year, for these fish would travel overland in the heavy morning dew, home they would be taken, for many country folk enjoyed a 'snig' (eel). I don't remember hearing of any being jellied, but apparently they are delicious fried, although I could never fancy them!

The River Dee, in its lower reaches, is a good coarse fishing river, but the children were not allowed to fish there, for its deep swirling waters are extremely danger-ous, claiming many lives over the years. Men spent summer evenings fishing in these, at times foreboding waters, never knowing what denizen of the deep was likely to take their enticing bait. It could be an eel, a fluke, roach, dace or even the occasional trout! Today the modern fisherman with modern tackle is usually fishing in a club match, a different (forgive this) kettle of fish, for there are usually prizes or money for the winner who has caught the heaviest weight.

154

Most of the hobbies enjoyed by adults had an end product. A woodman for instance would make baskets of various sizes and for various purposes. Ellis Thomas was an expert at this and of course his occupation gave him the opportunity to get the material he needed. Using the white withen, the gathering of which has been described earlier, Ellis would weave maybe a large basket for use when getting potatoes. This would be of the larger wands, and would last for a number of years. A smaller version, of a similar design, would be for apple or fruit gathering, and of course a popular basket was the one favoured by the women, the washing basket. Most of these are of course discontinued lines even when made of plastic. Shopping baskets were made for the women to use on their weekly shopping expeditions, but naturally they had to be a bit more refined than the working ones. Ellis used the red withen to give a splash of colour to the waxen shade of the white willow and he could weave quite intricate designs into a basket to be used for shopping, making a very attractive container for the ladies to fill at the local markets! These were, I must say, a much more pleasant sight than the hideous, advert-covered plastic carrier bags seen everywhere in such large numbers. It is doubtful if Ellis ever took any money for his creations for they were made as gifts. The material cost him nothing, and time was of no importance during the long winter evenings. Only recently I saw a basket hanging in a shed at an old friend's house, and when I asked about it I was told that Ellis Thomas had made it years ago. Now Ellis passed away over thirty years ago, and the basket, although rather dilapidated was still serviceable. To me it was an epitaph to Ellis's skill.

Some men of the woods, having every chance to find and choose the best material, would make walking sticks. Often they would spot a sapling of maybe ash, hardly large enough to make a stick, but this would be earmarked, and maybe two years later, collected and put to dry. The sticks could be made from many types of young growth, some would be simply trimmed and varnished, some not even varnished but smoothed down with fine sandpaper. Let's go through the various timbers used in the old country art of stick making. Different parts of the country have a predominance of one particular coppice growth; on the lighter chalky soils this is usually hazel, and on the heavier loams ash. Ash is a very tough but 'giving' wood, the thinner sticks being quite whippy. The woodmen might dig a young sapling up, and find, particularly on clay soil, that the root was at a right angle to the young shoot. This of course was ideal for it was a ready made handle, and only judicious trimming was required to make quite an attractive stick. A straight and not too thick sapling needed different treatment if it was to make a good walking stick, for it needed to be turned to create the handle. The stick maker would gather several suitable young growths, and arrange with the gamekeeper to be present when he had the boiler going, before mixing the pheasant feed. When the water was boiling madly, the sticks would be placed across the boiler in the mass of steam. After some time the wood would become quite malleable and then, with great care it would be bent around a circular object, usually a drain pipe. It had to be moulded into a suitable shape, without the bark being broken, and then it would be tied in that shape with strong string. Each shaped stick was then hung in an airy place for the wood to season, and in due course, when the string was removed and the stick trimmed and smoothed, it became a most useful object. Today ash plants are more or less mass produced, being grown for the purpose, but if you own an ash stick you will quite likely see the slight mark where the string has been tied to form the U of the handle. The same method as that used by the old woodmen has been employed.

Frank Milton was an expert at stick making, and having lived and worked on an estate all his life he could always obtain the raw material. Hazel sticks were his speciality, and some real masterpieces he turned out. He always gathered the sticks during the winter months, when the sap was low, and these would be stored in a well ventilated shed for probably twelve months to season. The handles were the attractive parts of Frank's sticks. He would make them out of various materials: stag horn, ram's horn, and boxwood. The horns were carved into unusual forms, and often the boxwood, being a most attractive yellow, was carved into birds' and animals' heads, this being truly a labour of love. When completed, the hazel sticks were always varnished, which brought out the various shades of the thin bark, ranging from a pale green to an almost chocolate brown. Frank called these sticks with the lifelike carved handles 'ceremonial sticks', for they were too good to use in the normal way. In fact many found their way into hall stands where they were purely decorative. Now and again a stick maker would come across a suitable sized sapling which had a creeper twisted around it and sometimes embedded in the bark. It was in most cases the wild honeysuckle, and its climbing habit would produce a lovely spiral of raised bark, a much sought after object. This occurred on both ash and hazel, but probably was at its best on a sturdy hazel.

Blackthorn bushes also provided good material, although in many cases sticks made from the young growth of a sloe bush were claimed to be blackthorn. Anyone with a knowledge of these matters could soon tell the difference, for the sloe sticks had lumps or raised spots throughout their length, some six inches apart. The true blackthorn, a rather rare bush in many areas, had long raised thorns at close intervals, and these were much more prominent than on the sloe. A good blackthorn stick always had as many of the savage thorns as possible left on it, and going back through the years this custom had a useful purpose. A traveller when accosted by a robber would raise his blackthorn as if attempting to hit his assailant, but instead of bringing the stick down he would allow the villain to grab it, preferably with both hands. At that precise moment the traveller, using considerable force, would draw the stick with its protruding thorns through the villain's hands. This would cause deep lacerations to the palms of the hands and the traveller would beat a hasty retreat, leaving his assailant in a state of distress. In fairly recent times the gamekeepers favoured such a stick in preference to a club, for it was a much more efficient tool.

Many other saplings were used to provide aids to walking in the country. White elm is a rather soft but light-weight wood, holly is heavy and difficult to carve, while yew is a tough timber. Then there is sweet chestnut, which is used to a large extent for shop bought sticks. When a sweet chestnut tree is felled in due course many young shoots will spring up from the seat. After a year or two these can be cut and they make useful sticks, particularly for ladies, for they can be stained and varnished in many attractive colours. The handle is bent in a similar way to the ash, the main difference being that the stick is heated over an open fire, which makes the wood pliable in the same way that steam does, but in this case the bark is removed. The bark peels off quite easily whilst the stick is hot, and this is done before the handle is tied in position.

All sticks must be seasoned in a light airy place, and are better kept in such conditions at all times. Many woodmen excelled at this hobby, and were very skilled both in selecting suitable subjects to work with and achieving a most attractive finish.

Wine has always been made in the country; perhaps this can hardly be classed as a hobby, but in some cases it was, for much experimenting would be done. Many things from rose petals to damsons would be used in an attempt to produce a drinkable liquid. Some of the results were all right but many were impossible. Wheat wine was popular with the farming community and if made properly was as potent as a malt whiskey. But like many of the brews of that time, it had a short storage life, perhaps because it was so good! As damsons were a heavy crop, damson wine was favoured by the cottagers. In one form this was supposed to be a cure for the common cold, although probably it was more of a relief, for it could be a potent fluid.

Many men would take a small bottle to work with them on a cold day, and I remember one occasion, a shooting day it was, when the game cart man, one Tom Broster, had a bottle with him. It was during that arctic winter of nineteen sixty three, with sub zero temperatures. Well into the morning's sport Tom produced his bottle to give his assistant a nip. Alec Minshull, the 'go-for' on the cart, took the cork out and put the bottle to his lips. After what seemed a long while Tom said 'Dunna sup it all mester,' and Alec replied, 'There's nowt in it.' Tom said, 'Well take the cork out.' 'The cork is out,' said Alec, and when the pair of them investigated further, they discovered that the wine was frozen solid! They didn't go without a drink though, for Tom put the cork back in, jammed the bottle behind the tractor radiator, and thawed the liquid out. I'm not sure of this but I thought a very low temperature was needed to freeze alcohol, so maybe there was a high proportion of juice in Tom's brew!

The wheat wine was often drunk at the meal provided by the farmer for his workers when the last load of the harvest was gathered. (This meal was not the true harvest supper which took place after the Church Thanksgiving Service, usually in the village hall). The farmer would provide an ample feed for his workers in appreciation of their good service and hard work, and the wheat wine naturally created an atmosphere of bonhomie. The workers were not paid overtime in those days, but were usually given a sum of money, perhaps not more than two pounds, and this often depended on whether the harvest had been a good one. A good feed at the farmer's expense was therefore much appreciated.

As I have said there was quite a bit of experimenting in an effort to produce a wine that was a palatable drink. Even the fruits used annually could vary from year to year and great care and skill was needed during the fermentation period. When something different was being processed, it was often a hit or miss affair. On one occasion a certain lady was trying something new. All had gone well and the wine had been bottled. The usual practice was to leave the corks in the bottles loose, so that should there be any excess gas it could escape. Then after a few days, when the wine had settled down, the corks would be pushed home tight.

The lady decided that no more gas was in the wine and so tightened the corks. All was well for a couple of days or so, then at night, when the household had retired and everyone was asleep, there was an explosion. 'Get up John' said the lady, 'Someone's shooting.' Up got John and proceeded warily down stairs holding a lighted candle in front of him, but nothing was to be seen or heard. 'You're dreaming woman,' John shouted upstairs. 'No I wasn't,' came the reply, 'Have a look around.' Well John, still treading carefully, looked in the kitchen, the pantry and the scullery, but found nothing. He then opened the wash-house door, and as he stepped inside there was a crunch of glass under his fortunately slippered feet. Glass! John stopped in his tracks, and then a strong fruity smell met his nostril. 'Ah that's it' he thought, 'That new brew has gone off and busted a bottle.' Back in bed he told his wife how daft she had been to get up to such tricks.

The next morning his wife came down stairs first (all country women were up first in those days), and went to see what had happened the previous night. What a mess! The full light of day revealed what couldn't be seen by a flickering candle. There was glass all over the place, and liquid still dripping from the shelves. Nearly all the bottles of experimental brew had exploded, maybe by chain reaction, and not only that, very few bottles of the traditional stuff were left on the shelf above! When John came down there was hell to pay. The winter supply had almost all been wasted, and he was most annoyed for he was fond of a glass of wine before 'going to roost' of a winter's night. No doubt, country folk being what they are, people would rally round and an odd bottle here and another there would ensure John's nightcap! News of such a calamity would travel fast.

It was rather noticeable in the prewar days that a country worker would have a hobby or pastime, or even a sport which was in some way connected with his full time employment. The hobbies of the basket maker and the stick maker have already been described. As a rule the gardeners kept their cottage gardens neat and tidy and always had good quality produce, no doubt because of the availability of plants! The farm workers, at least in many cases, tended to be a bit rough and ready, and could not attend to small details like pulling weeds! Tom Broster, a real character who I have already mentioned, worked on, and indeed spent most of his life on the estate golf course. He was a man of considerable girth and weight to go with it, as is illustrated by what happened once in a chip shop. Whilst waiting his turn to be served Tom popped a penny in the weighing machine. The machine weighed up to twenty stones, but when Tom got on, it went round with such force that there was a loud snapping sound, and the needle failed to return to zero! The proprietor of the chippy was furious and Tom had to beat a hasty retreat, without his feed of fish and chips.

That incident was a diversion, for my intention was really to write about golfing. Now Tom and his friend and workmate, one Fred Thomas, were wont to have a game of golf of a spring evening, and incidently were no mean players. This particular evening the pair were enjoying making their leisurely way round the nine hole course, and no doubt assessing any work that needed to be done in the future, when a figure appeared in the distance. Tom drove off the tee, a good straight long drive, but Fred pulled his shot a bit and was off the fairway in longer grass. The pair set off up the fairway, Fred turning off in the direction of his ball, whilst Tom kept straight on. Then the figure previously seen appeared from behind a huge oak tree, came up to Tom, and with hand outstretched said, 'I'm General Horrocks of Western Command.' Tom was taken aback, but being a quick wit replied, 'I'm Tom Broster of Aldford.' This rather amused the General, for it was indeed General Horrocks, and the round of golf had to be abandoned for a while as the pair talked about the army and war service. The following November the local

161

Ex-Servicemen's Dinner, of which Tom was chairman, was honoured by the presence of the General, and those present enjoyed his witty speech in reply to the toast to Her Majesty's Services. Tom Broster was a great character who unfortunately died at the comparatively young age of sixty-two, but his friend Fred though no longer a young man, still plays golf regularly.

Now it is essential, particularly in a rural area, that folk take part in the various organisations, ranging from, maybe a darts club in the local pub, to the Women's Institute, or even the Parish Council. All these organisations need committees, except of course the Parish Council, and it has become very noticeable over the years that the same limited number of people sit on a lot of committees! These good folk must really be treating all their activities as hobbies and pastimes, for there can be a lot of time and labour involved, not to mention the odd pound or two now and again.

A number of years ago, soon after the Second World War, a few chaps lately out of the Forces, got together and formed a committee, the idea being to have a really good bonfire on Guy Fawkes night. Throughout the war there had, of necessity, been no bonfires, let alone fireworks on this night, and even when the bonfire restrictions were lifted, fireworks were unobtainable. When the ex-servicemen got together, they were able to obtain a limited supply of roman candles, catherine wheels, rockets and jumping jacks. Most of the younger children had never seen a display of fireworks or even a large bonfire, so an organised event was to be a real treat. After a lot of discussion it was decided to order fourteen pounds' worth of assorted fireworks which was quite a lot in those days. The fire itself did not take a lot of organising, it was just a question of persuading the local farmers to cart their hedge trimmings to the chosen site, the pub field! The local garage was quite willing to supply some old sump oil, just to make sure when the time came, that the flames would roar heavenwards.

However a straightforward fire with fireworks was not an ambitious enough project for the lads, there had to be something more, despite the fact that they were starting

162

from scratch, without a penny in the kitty. 'Ah what about a torchlight procession' said one. 'Let's have Lally Huxley's band' said another, 'Don't forget this is for the kids' said the chairman, 'We must have a prize for the best Guy.' 'Well what about pop and crisps for 'em then' (the kids) said another chap, and so it went on. Nobody had any idea where the money was coming from, except from the collecting tins which would be much in evidence on the night.

The torches for the evening parade were probably the biggest headache, nobody knew how to make them. After some research the Hon. Secretary discovered that old hessian sacks wired tightly around the end nine inches of a green willow stick would, when soaked in a mixture of paraffin and diesel oil, last long enough for the parade. About fifty of these torches were needed, for many villagers wanted to take part. There was more cadging of fuel, and soon the torches, rough and ready as they were, were soaking up the inflammable liquid.

The night itself was a great occasion, practically all the village congregated at the pub, for the procession started there, and finished on the field opposite, after touring the village, a distance of three quarters of a mile. The band struck up and the marshals lit the torches. What a sight they made in the darkness of a dreary November evening. Sparks flew everywhere, but there was no danger, as it had rained as usual most of the day. The band played stirring marching tunes, and fortunately, folks, many of them from the surrounding villages, made the collecting tins rattle as they gave their contribution to the event.

The fire was lit by a retired Colonel who lived in the area, as the band played the regimental march of his old regiment, The Durham Light Infantry, something he didn't expect but greatly appreciated. The committee started letting off the fireworks whilst the crowd remained outside the roped-off area and when the rockets roared skywards, the cheers must have been heard in the next villages! The cattle in the farm buildings 'blarted' and the dogs barked, some children cried for they had never seen the like of this before, but when the pop and crisps were handed out, the children gathered round, crying or not. It was a great night which was repeated annually for quite a while, but now alas no more.

After that first night the committee had a meeting to study the financial situation, and the man in charge of these matters reported that there was a shortage of cash. He would need seven pence halfpenny from each of the committee members, and then the accounts would show a credit balance of one halfpenny! Of course all willingly paid up. In fact that organisation still organises events in the village, and the fund still has that odd halfpenny on its accounts! It has always been said that if you want anything to be done, get a busy man to do it, well all the men, and women involved in the event described were in full time employment working long hours. Service to the community was and is their hobby, one that must give a great feeling of satisfaction.

The hobbies and pastimes so far described have mostly been those of men, but we mustn't forget the women, God bless them. Although many of the things women used to do were in a way hobbies, they also served a useful and sometimes an essential purpose. As wages were rather low, anything that could boost them made a lot of difference to the living standards of the family. The women made jams, bottled fruit, and did many tasks with a needle. Maybe one lady would make 'rough aprons' as they called them, from hessian feed sacks, which would be worn whilst doing dirty work or even household chores, the fancy pinafore was for Sunday, not to work in! Another lady would maybe be an expert at making tea cosies, so a fair amount of swapping, or bartering, went on. Clothing was never wasted. It was the farmer's cast off worn out jacket that went on the 'mawkin' (scarecrow), not the worker's. Practically all clothing, when worn out, was used in some way. The women would cut almost any item into strips to make a multi-coloured rug, for either the hearth or the bedroom. These rugs would last for years, and by the time they showed signs of wear, enough strips of old clothing would be available to make another one. Farmers' wives also made these rugs of course, but the material in a prosperous farmer's clothing would be of a better quality. Once a farmer was asked what he did with his worn out jackets. 'What do ye think mon,' was the reply, 'I wears 'em.'

It was usually the women who gathered the fruits of the countryside, such as mushrooms, blackberries, eating chestnuts and crab apples. The small apple of the crab tree, which in some areas frequently flourished in hedges and woodsides, was made into crab apple jelly. There are many varieties of crab apple, but only the small rosy apples would be used, for they gave the jelly an attractive pink colour. The jelly would be on the table when one of the back yard roosters had the place of honour, or maybe when the odd game bird had found its way to that household! In fact crab apple jelly is as good as, and in the opinion of a lot of people, better than, red currant or cranberry.

Blackberries, always available in large quantities in the old days, were used in tarts and pies, and made into jam. They were often mixed with other fruits such as apples. Today this black luscious fruit is not so readily obtainable, for the modern hedgecutter used regularly year after year, does not allow the rambling briars to reach the fruiting stage. It is not wise, even where roadside hedges have been rather neglected and have a profusion of briars, and often a heavy crop of berries, to gather them. The fumes and dust sent up by the passing traffic contaminate the fruit, and although they are probably a long way from being toxic, they do not make for really palatable dishes. If you wish to gather any berries, you should obtain permission to enter a wood or land away from traffic. At least horses never polluted anything!

Mushrooms, although not to everybody's taste, have always been popular with country folk who have no problem in telling the true mushroom from any fungi. Even the larger version of the white capped, pink frilled mushroom, the 'horse' mushroom, is easily distinguished and often eaten. I was once walking a hedgerow, and came across an Irish labourer busy cleaning out the ditch. It was lunch time, and the Irishman was sitting by a small fire, and in his hands he held one of the largest mushrooms I have ever seen. As I was talking to him, he placed it on a thick forked stick, and held it over the clear fire. I watched this performance enthralled to see what would happen next. In a very short while, the centre of the dish-shaped mushroom started to fill with a brown coffee-like liquid – there must have been almost a pint of it. As it started to steam, the Irishman put the mushroom to his lips and drank the warm fluid. 'Now what's that like Paddy?' said I. 'To be sure you would no be knowing would you?' 'No, what is it like?' I replied. 'It be the next best thing to them there Liffy waters, I reckon' said Paddy, but I could not bring myself to taste the brew, so am in ignorance of its flavour to this day. I can only conjecture that it must have been similar to the mushroom ketchup that the women made when there was a glut, lovely in and on a shepherd's pie, but hardly as a drink I would think.

Mushrooms, that is the real ones, the wild mushrooms, are unpredictable things. There will be plenty one year, none the next, and a field that was covered with them one year will be bare when they are to be found everywhere else. The farm workers always knew where they were of course. One September many years ago, one of the men had been back to the farm to 'look up' some cows due to calve, and as it was dark and late before he finished his task, he took a short cut home. As he was crossing a field off his regular route, he came across the odd white circle in the grass. He took little notice having had many feeds of mushrooms in recent weeks. Then the circles became more numerous, until he had great difficulty in putting his feet down without treading on one. When he got to his cottage he told his wife about the quantity of mushrooms on the Glebe field. 'Like saucers every one of 'em,' said George. 'Well we baint letting them lot spoil,' said his wife. 'Get the clothes basket.' So the pair set out and on reaching the field proceeded to fill the huge wicker container with perfect even-sized mushrooms. It wasn't long before the basket was piled high, and as George was holding one handle and his wife the other, they had difficulty in walking without shedding some of the load! 'What you going to do with this lot?' George said to his wife Eadie. 'Sell 'em of course, what do you think. You've had plenty and these 'ere be too good to waste.' The next morning Eadie was busy transferring the mushrooms into large

166

cardboard boxes so that the weekly carrier could pick them up, for by sheer chance it was the day he passed on his way to town. The white cloth was in the window to indicate that he should call, and before long he did. 'Take these to so-and-so's,' said Eadie, 'and dunna ye get pinching a feed, I've weighed 'em' (which she hadn't). 'Drop me the money off when you come back, I'll pay ye then,' Eadie carried on. The carrier called late that afternoon and handed Eadie a sealed envelope, 'That's it', the carrier said, 'Give us a bob and we'll call it right.' When he had departed, Eadie with some haste tore open the envelope, to examine its contents. Two pounds twelve and sixpence she found, almost a pound more than George her husband brought home each week. When George got home that evening there was twelve and sixpence at his place at the table. 'That's your share of the mushroom money,' Eadie remarked, 'and don't spend it all on beer and baccy, I wants a new pair of shoes for me birthday.' In those days a pair of shoes cost around seven and sixpence, baccy was eight pence an ounce, and beer four pence a pint so even George seemed quite well off.

Many such incidents happened in the countryside and in these chapters I have endeavoured to recall some characters I have known and some of the things they did and also to describe a few of the skills required in their various jobs. Many of these skills are no longer used, nor the tools that went with them. A few, such as hedgelaying linger on, and the finished job is a joy to behold. Some of the things described did not and do not need much skill, gathering mushrooms for instance, but even here a knowledge of the countryside is a great asset.

Life cannot stand still, nature never stands still, there is always change. Some changes are for the better, and some not, but who knows, should we look to the past to see the future?